T0114771

RACIAL
RECONCILIATION

A Theological Approach to Building Relationships

DR. CALVIN GLASS

WESTBOW
PRESS®
A DIVISION OF THOMAS NELSON
& ZONDERVAN

This book is a work of non-fiction. Unless otherwise noted, the author
and the publisher make no explicit guarantees as to the accuracy of
the information contained in this book and in some cases, names of
people and places have been altered to protect their privacy.

WestBow Press books may be ordered through booksellers or by contacting:

WestBow Press
A Division of Thomas Nelson & Zondervan
1663 Liberty Drive
Bloomington, IN 47403
www.westbowpress.com
844-714-3454

Because of the dynamic nature of the Internet, any web addresses or
links contained in this book may have changed since publication and
may no longer be valid. The views expressed in this work are solely those
of the author and do not necessarily reflect the views of the publisher,
and the publisher hereby disclaims any responsibility for them.

Any people depicted in stock imagery provided by Getty Images are
models, and such images are being used for illustrative purposes only.
Certain stock imagery © Getty Images.

ISBN: 978-1-6642-9759-3 (sc)
ISBN: 978-1-6642-9758-6 (hc)
ISBN: 978-1-6642-9466-0 (e)

Library of Congress Control Number: 2023907016

Print information available on the last page.

WestBow Press rev. date: 04/18/2023

CONTENTS

ABBREVIATIONS

BBR	Building Better Relationships
DMIN	Doctor of Ministry
GDP	Greater Detroit Partnership
HCA	His Church Anglican
LUSOD	Liberty University School of Divinity
LOLCC	Lord of Lords Christian Church
MU	Ministers United

Bibles

AMP	The Amplified Bible
KJV	The King James Version
MESG	The Message Bible
NIV	The New International Version
NKJV	The New King James Version
NLT	The New Living Translation
TLV	The Tree of Life Version

PREFACE

Racism within the Christian community in America has resulted in social unrest and has plagued the Christian church in a way that mandates urgent solutions to this untamed malady. This book's focus is on learning a practicable methodology based on biblical principles that address racial reconciliation (building God-approved relationships with all ethnic groups) that will combat racial disunity and disconnect among Christians. The study method used BBR (Building Better Relationships), which consisted of interviewing and teaching focus groups representing a Black Christian congregation, a non-Black Christian congregation, and a group of local diverse senior pastors and ministers in the metro Detroit area. The focus-group participants received teaching and training on biblical racial reconciliation directives through a six-session curriculum and bimonthly meetings. Ten individuals—five Black Christian leaders and five non-Black Christian leaders—made up the first two focus groups. Another group of local Christian leaders made up the third group. The objective of the research was to describe the reality of historical racism in the Christian community and to motivate and implement multicultural change that will enhance the building of theologically healthy and loving relationships among all races (ethnic groups).

Dr. Calvin Glass's life, ministry, and passion are dedicated to ensuring that Christians worldwide experience the reality of building intimate relationships with God through His Son Jesus Christ, and know the transferable anointing of the Holy Spirit as it relates to the God-ordained ministry of reconciliation that every believer should demonstrate with God and His created world. In this book, you will learn a theological perspective for racial reconciliation and a practical and workable methodology that will bring racial healing to the Body of Christ and the world we serve.

ACKNOWLEDGMENTS

I would like to express my gratitude to my wife Nina, our eight children; Pastors Melvin and Sandy Gower; my mentor, Dr. Zabloski, Lord of Lords congregation; Pastor Allen and His Church Anglican congregation; the pastors and leaders of Ministers United and Greater Detroit Partnership; the research participants; and all my family members and friends who encouraged me that racial reconciliation was a theme worth researching.

MY WINDOW OF PAIN

There are many ways of observing life
With the Joy of things that remain.
Yet I grasp a different sight
Of a well-structured window of pain.

These undeserved barriers keep men apart
Separating the Land of the Free.
A reality of this mindless heart
Has destroyed much dignity.

Why is there such a frame?
Where Love doesn't seem to count
But hate is shown unfeignedly so,
Promoting countless doubts.

The more I look, the more I see
The problems we must face.
Despite the many progresses
Of my vigilant race.

Blame it on lost history
Or even those of the past.
But don't you think the one to blame
Is he who blocks freedom's path?

The soldier knows what he must do
To win against his foes,
And bring them to a point of defeat
Through judgment, truth, and woes.

So I stand in total dejection
Hoping for positive change.
Asking God for a better revelation
Of my unwanted window of pain.

Calvin Glass

INTRODUCTION

Since the origin of civilization, humanity's identity and imagery have been challenged, distorted, and debated. Authentic conversations concerning racial reconciliation, race status, and race relations are still among the most curious, misunderstood, and researched subjects of modern academia. As the Christian church faces the many struggles of modernity, the age-old fight for true racial unity and harmony still lingers as a major thorn in the flesh. My research for this book identifies my pure motive and desire to implement biblical truths that will change unbiblical thinking and behavior when it comes to race relations. My optimistic pursuit is that the battle for racial reconciliation among most Christians is in alignment with Jesus's prayer for Christian unity. In the Lord's Prayer, he said,

> My prayer is not for them alone. I pray also for those who will believe in me through their message, that all of them may be one, Father, just as you are in me and I am in you. May they also be in us that the world may believe that you have sent me. I have given the glory that you gave me, that they may be one as we are one: I in them and you in me. May they be brought to complete unity to let the world know that you sent me and have loved them even as you have loved me. (John 17:20–23, NIV)

Many other scriptures in the Bible (some we will discuss) encourage multiethnic oneness and promote intentional human efforts toward real congregational and social fellowships among Christ's followers and the world we serve. This research process is to examine racial reconciliation from a historical and theological perspective with a core focus to bring collaboration and methodology to the Christian community that will help all races to live with divine truth and harmonious affirmations.

Christians possess a moral compass that, if used, effectively establishes a model of ethical goals and behaviors that has the potential to improve race relations in the Christian community and the world. Our public profession of faith in Christ Jesus will always advance Christ's agenda and purpose on earth. The conceivability of kingdom unity connected to a Christian biblical worldview dictates the proper functioning of the Christian who has accepted his/her call to become Christ's ambassador for his reconciliation ministry. The kingdom ambassador's job is crucial for end-time ministry and must be understood as urgent work. Establishing the trust factor among races that will set standards for unselfish norms and practices resulting in respect and care for each other is a core ingredient of this work. This book can lead you to a deeper look at this complicated transforming ministry. As you read this book, keep in mind that there are some traditional values and unbiblical privileges among Christians that require a new level of investigation and attention. These new eyes can lead to a bolder initiative that challenges a code of conduct and recommends a serious call for aggressive leadership training and modeling.

The solution to racial disparities within the Christian community must propose key disciplines that remedy obtained knowledge and the biblical-based mobilization of truth. The charge of scriptures for the kingdom ambassador on improving racial relations and the move of the Holy Spirit within the lives of the transformed believers are the ingredients for connectional fellowship, unconditional love, and freedom from many forms of bondage. The immediate results of racial reconciliation teaching have brought about a high level of expectancy for change among the students and a hunger to meet individual and congregational needs by creating an environment where mistakes are not fatal and where collaboration is encouraged, recognized, and applauded. The removal of racial manipulation will help the Christian leader to persuade their congregants to do something that may be uncomfortable and unpopular but worth the time and effort invested. This high-morale partnership calls for contagious enthusiasm glued to theological hope, which is the foundational tool for achieving kingdom unity as a divinely prescribed accomplishment. The challenge to serve God, support a worthy socialization cause, and, at the same time, honor all races is the proper kingdom agenda for multiethnic success. My understanding is that we should not separate antiracism from the biblical ministry of reconciliation.

MY MINISTRY CONTEXT

Lord of Lords Christian Church (LOLCC) in Detroit, Michigan, began on January 16, 1990, as a church plant under the leadership of my dad, Pastor Clyde Glass Sr., and the King of Kings Missionary Baptist Church of Detroit. This church plant began as, and still is, a predominantly all-Black congregation. The location is on the east side of Detroit, the inner city, where low-income families reside. This area contends with a weak educational system, high unemployment, prisoner reentry concerns, and single-parenting homes, to name a few of our challenges. It is considered one of the top crimes, gang-related, disadvantaged environments in the United States.

The congregation is outreach-oriented, in that we provide groceries and clothes weekly to close to fifty families. The ministry is known for its neighborhood cleanup efforts, meeting the needs of seniors, back-to-school supplies for the neighborhood children, distributing turkeys for Thanksgiving Day, and bikes and toys for the Christmas season. These programs are essential programs that engage the Christian community to address social needs with the collaboration of community stakeholders. The educational level of the average congregant is under a four-year college-degree level. This limits the benefits of professionalism that many suburban Christian congregations enjoy. The heartbeat of the congregational life points toward discipleship orientation and implementation of diversified socialization. The discipleship program teaches the pupils to represent a moral and loving Creator God on earth. This is the biblical approach to racial reconciliation called the Great Commission found in the last chapter of the book of Matthew. "And Jesus came and spoke to them saying, all authority is given unto me in heaven and on earth. Go therefore and make disciples of all the nations, baptizing them in the name of the Father and of the Son and of the Holy Spirit, teaching them to observe all things that I have commanded you; and lo, I am with you always, even to the end of the age" (Matthew 28:18–20, NKJV). The instruction for the disciple of Christ is to focus on spreading the gospel of Christ's kingdom and to make disciples for Jesus Christ in every nation ("ethnos," every ethnic group).

Luke expanded on Jesus's instructions that he gave to his disciples before his ascension. Jesus told them, "You shall receive power when the Holy Spirit has come upon you; and you shall be witnesses to Me in Jerusalem, and in all Judea and Samaria, and to the end of the earth" (Acts 1:8, NKJV). Making disciples for Jesus Christ of every race was Christ's focus. Deviating from his core ingredient for kingdom expansion and his roadmap to cross-culture communication has resulted in the racial crisis we are facing today. This methodology for racial harmony that our congregation has now embraced again is by far the best solution for racial disconnect. There is a lot of work ahead for us because we, like most Christian congregations, detoured from this Christological strategy and have limited ourselves as community leaders as a real model for kingdom unity.

Another key component of utilizing this model reveals the

importance of leader/follower bonding. Positive pastor/member chemistry is the solution to path-goal deliveries—meaning that with a high need for mutual achievement, key individuals within the congregation must have personal stimulation before forward progress is assured.[1] The discipleship training mandates that each active member is encouraged biblically through congregational leadership. The teacher/pupil engagement and focus are to pursue and develop a Christian character through a spiritual formation that leads to a Christlike identity and lifestyle that impacts not only the individual but also the environment he or she serves. This lifestyle is to be learned and duplicated as a discipleship mandate.

It must be noted that the prioritization of leadership values and concerns in the congregation context determines, in no small part, the reactionary climax in the pews for social change and moral correctness. Two critical elements of this concept are that individuals who support the church leaders look to be formally rewarded and emotionally supported.[2] Secondly, the overall church impact goes hand in hand with the successful discipleship and modeling of each member of the congregation. This model (right or wrong) results from the culturally driven religious teaching of the lead pastor.

The call to follow and demonstrate Christ in the community should be crucial for the local Christian congregation. The focus must be on God's plan and purpose carried out for the world to see his glory and his power manifested within the community.[3] The urban church, historically, has sought to connect with other cultural experiences in the hope that pluralism becomes some form of beauty

---

[1] Sikandar Hayyat Malik, "A Study of Relationship Between Leader-Behaviors and Subordinate Job Expectancies: A Path-Goal Approach," *Society for Personal Research* vol. 6 no. 2 (2012): 361.

[2] Jiaxin Huang, Lin Wang, and Jun Xie, "Leader-Member Exchange and Organizational Citizenship Behavior: The Roles of Identification with Leader and Leader's Reputation," *Social Behavior and Personality* 42 no.10 (2014): 1703.

[3] Paul Cannings, *Making Your Vision A Reality: Proven Steps to Develop and Implement Your Church Vision Plan* (Grand Rapids: Kregel Publications, 2013), 77.

and diversity in some kind of stimulation. However, the pursuit of racial unity among many Christians in the past has hindered progress. This study assumes that there is limited involvement within the history of Christianity that honestly emphasizes an accurate assessment, mutual academic and theological agreement, and historical activities concerning building positive race identities and relationships by the majority of past Christian leaders. This has been my research migraine. Furthermore, any plan for capacity building in the future is known to fail if it does not incorporate the needs and strengths of all parties.[4] I believe that leadership in the pulpit and the followership in the pews demonstrating the loving heart and mind of Christ has a unique opportunity to advance racial reconciliation principles not only within the walls of our houses of worship but also within the broader diverse Christian community. I just don't see enough of it.

The researcher (author) holds the title of senior pastor of Lord of Lords Ministries. We as a Christian institution have served our inner-city community for over thirty-two years. Our individual, as well as church, life experiences, and other social and cultural concerns, validated the need for further pursuit of and research on racial reconciliation among all Christians. I am also one of the chartered members of the Greater Detroit Partnership (GDP). This organization focuses on training pastors to develop meaningful and productive relationships cross-culturally with each other. The coordinators of the organization help the senior pastors in the group to develop a practical and workable approach to racial reconciliation for leadership in congregations, the regional Christian community, and the world.

Minister's United (MU), an organization I established in 2000, is a platform for lay leaders, ministers, and pastors to get training in racial reconciliation, kingdom unity, and ministry outreach by connecting the congregational leaders with other

---

[4] Victoria C. Scott and Susan M. Wolfe, *Community Psychology: Foundations for Practice* (Los Angeles: SAGE Publications, Inc., 2015), 193.

like-minded leaders and community stakeholders who have access to resources for economic justices and moral enhancements. GDP meets monthly for training, prayer, and fellowship with a group of diversified pastors. This organization also encourages deepening those cross-culture relationships outside of the monthly meetings and among their congregants. MU meets quarterly to focus on individual and community needs and to have presentations that will help connect ministers who have the same purpose of developing positive culture transformation, moral collaboration, and economic justice. Thrivent action teams, Meijer, Henry Ford Health Ministers, Lighthouse of Roseville, Focus Hope, Council for Baptist Pastors, Convoy of Hope, Faith Works, Life Remolded, Bikes4Kids, Michigan Interfaith Power & Light, and Detroit 2030 District are some of the organizations that have been active partners with Lord of Lords outreach programs.

MY STUDY

Racial reconciliation is a controversial subject that needs additional research and discussion. It has a biblical foundation that complements diversity and unity among humans. The Christian community can play a vital role in improving race relations and how it affects socialization issues such as racism, poor education, single parenting, police brutality, mass incarceration, systematic injustices, and high unemployment. The failure to understand and appropriate God's plan of righteousness and justice for all peoples in the Christian community and the world is the reconciliation minister's challenge. The psalmist Ethan the Ezrahite wrote, "Righteousness and justice are the foundation of your throne; Unfailing love and truth walk before you as attendants" (Psalm 89:14, NLT).[5] Undertaking this road of investigating race relations and implementing God's unconditional love within the Christian community and the world is a road that has been and still is critically examined and is now sensitively managed by various cultural and doctrinal positions. Most of these perspectives seem to hurt more than help the goal of racial unity.

Some inclinations from this research overshadow positive attitudes toward antiracism. For example, I have learned that even a gesture of biblical and spiritual correction has traditionally lost

---

[5] The four attributes that represent God's actions on this earth and among his children are righteousness, justice, love, and truth.

out to criticism and unsympathetic attitudes toward minorities and others who seek a change among clueless churchism. Past humiliation and systemic injustices have played an important role in promoting disunity and disconnect within America's Christianity. Politics that plague or punish the Christian community for wanting to and knowing how to transform into a multiracial community for positive modeling has become a modern malady. Furthermore, a challenge to eliminate racism among Christians is not a new vision but a renewed Christological hope. If we want real and lasting oneness, we must support the efforts of activist stakeholders that carry the baton for true racial reconciliation. With the Bible as the guidebook and compass for genuine change, a revolutionary evolution continues to emerge as a divine strategy. These research findings mentioned in this book suggest that the history of well-meaning visions and thoughts that promises racial reconciliation success has fallen short, with noticeable limitations and outright failure of fulfilling Christ's prayer for corporate unity.

The good thing to grasp is that the discussion about improving racial relations within the Christian community and the world is escalating daily at an alarming rate. The debate for remedies has center stage in the pews, news, and media outlets. Many new authors have risen to the occasion while pioneers of reconciliation ministry now possess a renewed faith. This urgent godly priority demands moral empathy, righteous indignation, and the most effective course of action that can implement an effective plan for racial unity and reconciliation. It is this moral high ground, this biblical plan of God that has been lost or rejected but now demands immediate consideration. The problem that this research identified is that most Christian communities and congregations may not want and/or understand the theological basis for racial reconciliation.

PURPOSE STATEMENT

There are many scriptures and narratives in the Bible that address racial/ethical reconciliation and its many fundamental elements. Jonah struggled with the calling and the command of God to be a blessing to the people of Nineveh. Jonah 1:1–3 (NKJV) reported, "Now the word of the Lord came to Jonah the son of Amittai, saying 'Arise, go to Nineveh, that great city, and cry out against it; for their wickedness has come up before me.' But Jonah arose to flee to Tarshish from the presence of the Lord. He went down to Joppa, and found a ship going to Tarshish; so, he paid the fare, and went down into it, to go with them to Tarshish from the presence of the Lord." Instead of obeying God's instructions to go and preach to Nineveh, Jonah fled to Tarshish in disobedience to God's desire for him to be a blessing to a non-Jewish nation. The narrative further explained that Jonah was thrown overboard from the boat by the boat officials. Jonah ended up in the belly of a large fish, where he prayed to God and repented for his disobedience. God then gave Jonah another chance to demonstrate divine love and grace to the Ninevites (chapters 2–3). This time Jonah ministered to Nineveh, repentance followed, and God blessed the land of the Ninevites. Still, Jonah became more hateful and delusional because God's blessings were for a non-Jewish nation. Jonah showed an attitude and mindset of racial (ethnic) superiority. "Then God saw their [Nineveh] works, that they turned from their evil way; and God relented from the disaster that He had said He would bring upon them and he did not do it. But it displeased Jonah exceedingly, and he became angry. So, he prayed to the Lord, and said, 'Ah, Lord, was not this what I said when I was still in my country? Therefore, I fled previously to Tarshish; for I know that you are a gracious and merciful God, slow to anger and abundant in lovingkindness, One who relents from doing harm'" (Jonah 3:10–4:2, NKJV). Jonah's attitude toward a non-Jewish nation was in opposition to the God of the universe who created all ethnic groups and who unconditionally loves all people.

Jesus astonished some of his Jewish followers (disciples) while showing compassion for another ethnic group by ministering to a Samaritan woman (John 4). He had mentioned the need to go through Samaria (v. 4) even though Jews had no dealings with Samaritans (v. 9). Jesus's conversation with this racially mixed Jewish woman confused the disciples because ethnic tensions and disunity were a way of life between the Jews and the Samaritans at that time. Another biblical narrative that reflects ethnic (racial) division is when Simon, a Cyrenian, carried Jesus's cross (Matthew 27:32). This Cyrenian helped to carry Jesus's cross because of the orders of the soldiers of the governor; this order came from non-Jewish soldiers. These examples of ethnic/racial disunity in the Bible (and there are many others) validate the premise that it is the will of God that racial oneness become of paramount importance in the heart of every believer. The purpose of this book is to teach the Christian community the theological basis for oneness and the need for racial reconciliation among one another that will impact the world we serve.

BASIC ASSUMPTIONS

The investigation of several scriptures in the Bible concludes that every believer in Christ ought to be committed to the ministry of reconciliation. For example, Luke gives us an account of Philip's cross-culture mission assignment on a desert road from Jerusalem to Gaza, he wrote, "Now an angel of the Lord said to Philip, go south to the road-the desert road-that goes down from Jerusalem to Gaza, so he started out, and on his way, he met an Ethiopian eunuch, an important official in charge of all the treasury of Candace queen of the Ethiopians. This man had gone to Jerusalem to worship" (Acts 8:26–27, NIV). That conversation resulted in

Philip giving a correct Old Testament interpretation of scripture concerning the Messiah, a deeper understanding of the Messiah's Samaritan mission, and the Christian conversion of the Ethiopian eunuch. Paul explained that God had empowered the Christian believer with the ministry of reconciliation. He wrote, "If anyone is in Christ, he is a new creation; the old has gone, the new has come! All this is from God, who reconciled us to himself through Christ and gave us the ministry of reconciliation" (2 Corinthians 5:17–18, NIV). Thus, making the Spirit-led believer an agent for radical change who will seek to connect the representation of all races of people into the Christian community. This is the mission of the reconciliation minister.

However, history concurs that there have been many past attempts to disassemble systemic racial inequalities and ethnic biases in the world and American Christianity with little to no real progress. Furthermore, the Black community and other minorities remain victims of hidden levels of deception consenting to various forms of institutional racism.[6] There needs to be a deeper understanding of scripture as it relates to racial reconciliation and the duplication of Christ's passion for expanding God's kingdom on earth. I have written this book with a justified urgency and a cry for effective social change. This book represents my attempt to provide a method involving a resurgence of biblical principles and a strategy for outreach theory that transforms the Christian mindset (if needed) with the application of divine love for all people on this earth.

The revealed fundamental challenge facing the American Christian community today is a concern that there has not been a lasting adequate and effective method to eliminate racial disparity within the Christian ranks. This challenge, in my opinion, has come to fruition. The many thriving past agendas that were labeled as help contributed to an increase in the division, disharmony,

[6] Henry Bettenson and Chris Maunder, *Documents of the Christian Church* 4th ed. (New York: Oxford University Press, 2011), 453.

and depression relating to the present-day racial tensions in the Christian world.

Moreover, effective Christianity must continue to address the need to eradicate mental health issues that stem from racial identity abuse and breakdown. The present mindset that's found in many Christian organizations and communities in America is a significant and compelling voice that affirms and demands racial reconciliation. However, as a misunderstood issue, racial reconciliation theology breeds enormous racial tension and contention within the larger Christian community. Therefore, I suggest, with unmovable optimism, that the solvability of the race problem lies in the hands of the most victimized—the Black Christian congregation.

I'm convinced that the Black Christian community must take ownership of the solution, mastery of specific knowledge, and affirmation of moral intelligence. Combating the negative trend of racial supremacy will result in new knowledge gained and interpreted to represent a new set of attitudes and skills that can be applauded and embraced by non-Black Christians. Moreover, it is this trend that articulates biblical truth, characterizes multiethnic traditions, and destroys theological errors. Nothing encourages the racial reconciliation facilitator more than real change toward real progress that embraces and realizes real racial unity. Spiritual change agents are the ones who see Christian households, communities, businesses, para-church organizations, and congregations as the central hubs for this moral redemption.

This passion for social change calls for strategic intentionality, verbal instructions, and skills that focus on justice, reformation, and transformation involving all races. Combating racial dysfunction and understanding the reasons why it exists sets the agenda in society for the elimination of other issues, such as violence, drugs, and criminal activities. It challenges systems that perpetuate poverty, hatred, unemployment, and injustices in the world. The spiritual and historical worlds can truthfully connect when truth prevails. Racial reconciliation cannot be just a thought—it must be a process that is reachable and solution-driven for all Christians to embrace. Regardless of what side of the racial problem you identify with, the core ingredient must be hope for change in a spirit of love and compassion.

The Bible is multiracial and multicultural, exposing a loving God whose aim is not to condemn the world, but through Jesus Christ, to deliver it from the bondage of all sin and its destructive results. John 3:16–17 (NIV) says, "For God so loved the world that he gave his one and only Son, that whoever believes in him shall not perish but have eternal life. For God did not send his Son into the world to condemn the world, but to save the world through him." Matthew 1:21 (TLV) reinforces this universal gospel perspective with the report that Mary would give birth to a son named Yeshua (Jesus) and that he would save his people from their sins. Both verses establish the heart of God as it relates to His passion for true reconciliation with all of mankind. Keep in mind, that certain narratives in the Bible have been taken out of their textual meaning to justify pretentious racial epitaphs, which was never the mindset of God or the biblical writer.

For example, when Jesus called the Canaanite woman a dog (Matthew 15:21–28), there was no sign of cultural disrespect, but there was a focus on ethnic preference and divine priority. "Leaving that place, Jesus withdrew to the region of Tyre and Sidon. A Canaanite woman from that vicinity came to him, crying out, 'Lord Son of David, have mercy on me! My daughter is suffering terribly from demon possession'" (vv. 21–22, NIV). The narrative records that Jesus did not answer her quickly and that Jesus's disciples urged him to send her away. Jesus then replied to the woman, "I was sent only to the lost sheep of Israel (v. 24) ... It is not right to take the children's bread and toss it to their dogs" (v. 26). The Canaanite woman, even though she was a Gentile, responded with true worship and unwavering faith, "Lord, help me!" Jesus then responded by declaring that her request was granted (v. 28).

The word *dog* in the English language can mean "a worthless person." It was used by Jesus to describe the ethnic bias that was real between the Jews and Gentiles of his day. He pointed out her level of boldness and faith as a Gentile woman (a person of another gender and race). Nowhere in the text did Jesus deem this woman worthless; instead, there was great respect given to this woman: "O woman, great is your faith" said Jesus (v. 28, NIV). He was, in this text, alluding to the ethnic and social division between Jews and Gentiles, which is still a challenge for his disciples today. Jesus used sarcasm to identify the distinctive character of the Jew (children's bread) and a nonconformist lot of the Gentiles (even the dogs). I believe that the heart of Christ is to point out deep-seated arrogance and inappropriate societal norms that hinder godly love from reaching its goal of improving relations between ethnic groups.

Racial tension can develop and has been developed through the misrepresentation of scripture and misinterpretation of actual biblical narratives. A slave mentality, psychologically damaging academia, false spirituality, and strained race relationships are some of the destructive results of historical inaccuracies. According to Lee June, "It is extremely important psychologically to recognize that Blacks were involved with Christianity long before the American sojourn in mass numbers because if we do not recognize the rich history of achievements prior to America, then we will have primarily a "slave mentality" and this can damage us psychologically."[7] Another focus of this research is to affirm that there are biblical texts that endorse the repair of damaged relationships among Christians, and this deeper understanding of reconciliation ministry represents the accuracy of God's loving mind and heart to bring healing and restoration among all humans. I assume that false historical narratives and doctrine among some scholars and academic influencers have led to greater racial tensions and sinful behavior adopted and taught by Christian leaders. The

[7] June, 24.

evidence is based on the misunderstanding, misinterpretation, and wrongful application of certain scriptures. For example, the biblical account of Jesus with the Samaritan woman (John 4) has been used to validate Christ's endorsement of institutionalized racism, which is not the heart of Christ.

A closer examination of the text can prove that Jesus focused on cultural tensions and contrasting beliefs that were prevalent between the Jews and the Samaritans at that time. I see also in this text solid principles for regional evangelism. The history of the Jews and Samaritans began after King Solomon's death. God's people were divided into two kingdoms: the northern part was called Israel, and the southern part was called Judah. Jeroboam and Rehoboam ruled Israel and Judah, respectively. Samaria was Israel's capital and Jerusalem was Judah's capital. After the invasion of the Northern Kingdom by the Assyrians, those who were left behind intermarried with Gentiles and worshipped foreign gods. Strong tension and disregard existed between the two ethnic groups. According to Merrill C. Tenney, "When the descendants of the southern captivity returned from Babylon in 539 B.C. to renew their worship under the Law, they found a complete rift between themselves and the inhabitants of Samaria, both religiously and politically."[8] He went on to write "By the time of Jesus a strong rivalry and hatred prevailed."[9] This religious and political breakdown is what Jesus addressed in the conversation with the Samaritan woman. She said, "Jews do not associate with Samaritans" (John 4:9, NIV), and Jesus explained to her, "You Samaritans worship what you do not know; we worship what we do know, for salvation is from the Jews" (v. 22, NIV). The disciples were surprised to see Jesus talking to this Samaritan woman (v. 27). The ethnic tension that existed among the Jews and the Samaritans was based on different styles of worship, cultural bias, and beliefs.

Bobby Griffith explained how the theology of race emerged:

---

[8] Tenney, 54.
[9] Ibid.

"We may think that theology adapts to practice, but it is not that simple. Sometimes, the complex interaction between culture, belief, economics, and social practices works in such a way that incorrect ideologies are promoted by even the most pious Christians."[10] I contend that the concept of biblical racial segregation theology must once and for all be destroyed based on the knowledge of the truth and the proper investigation and interpretation of reconciliation scriptures.

DEFINITIONS

Within the scope of this study, the words *race* and *racial* denote ethnic identity and cultural distinctiveness. The word *racism* suggests that one race is deemed superior to other nationalities in attitude and actions and that different nationalities are inferior and of lesser quality. The word *reconciliation* is a biblical term and concept that describes a restoration or renewal of relationships. It implies an intensive mutual change—i.e., from one person to another. It explains how "God was reconciling the world to himself in Christ" (2 Corinthians 5:19), resulting in Christ building and establishing his community on earth and giving them "the ministry of reconciliation" (2 Corinthians 5:18; Matthew 16:13–20). Reconciliation is defined as objective or provisional (before one is saved) and subjective or experimental (when one believes in God).[11] Christian and kingdom "unity" expresses my goal and understanding of racial reconciliation. It is the desired goal of every enlighten and empowered reconciliation minister.

Some words have been used improperly in the past that must be clarified. According to Mark Crear, the word *prejudice* means "a negative attitude or affective response toward a certain group

[10] Serven, 146.
[11] Paul Enns, *The Moody Handbook of Theology* (Chicago: Moody Publishers, 2008), 336.

and its individual members"; the word *stereotypes* means "beliefs about attributes that are thought to be characteristic of members of particular groups"; and the word *discrimination* means "unfair treatment of members of a particular group." Crear summarizes that "prejudice is an attitude, a stereotype is a belief, and discrimination is a treatment."[12] Understanding the definitive roots of racism and prejudices is key to behavioral change. According to Crear, three components identify all types of prejudices: "a cognitive component, which comprises a set of beliefs about the group or individual; an affective component, which is a feeling toward the group or individual; and a behavioral component, which is a set of behaviors or actions directed toward the group or individual based on the other two components."[13] A change of behavior is the result of a change in perspective thinking. New fortified Bible-based knowledge is the power for social change when applied with the spirit of reconciliation.

The exhortations to a Christlike humility are core to the work of reconciliation. A foundational scripture for reconciliation is found in Paul's letter to the Philippians: "If you have any encouragement from being united with Christ, if any comfort from his love, if any fellowship with the Spirit, if any tenderness and compassion, then make my joy complete by being like-minded, having the same love, being one in Spirit and purpose" (Philippians 2:1–2, NIV). Christian harmony has four fundamental principles that can relate to accomplishing racial reconciliation: (1) there is a certain consolation in Christ, (2) there is a certain comfort of love, (3) there is a specific fellowship of the Spirit, and (4) there are particular bowels and mercies.[14] The fundamental foundation for this book and my research rest on the researcher's interpretation and the participant's understanding of these terms.

---

[12] Mark Crear, *The Care and Counsel Bible* (Nashville: Thomas Nelson, 2001), 1646.
[13] Ibid.
[14] Kenneth Wuest, *Wuest's Word Studies: From the Greek New Testament* vol. 3 (Grand Rapids: Wm. B. Eerdmans Publishing Company, 1973), 109–112.

LIMITATIONS

When individuals cannot rightly interpret environmental values and belief systems, an alternative understanding of reality emerges. This research seeks to locate the underlying causes that affect change in understanding divine intelligence and explore new avenues of learning to better the Christian community in race relations. A sample survey (questionnaire) addressing the level of biblical knowledge of the selected congregational focus groups on racial relations and reconciliation was the aim. The focus-group participants were selected from the leadership of two congregations, Lord of Lord's Ministries and His Church Anglican these leaders were selected by their senior pastors. A questionnaire for the focus groups concerning the need for the development and implementation of relationship building within the Christian community produced the needed brainstorming for racial healing and the destruction of racial reconciliation demoralization within our ministries and communities. The number of participants in this questionnaire was limited to adult individuals (at least eighteen years of age) who volunteered and accepted the research qualifications and process.

Sampling all Christians was beyond the scope of this research. The findings reflected the thoughts and attitudes of diverse Christians within the region of the Lord of Lords Ministries. This approach dictated the aspirations of a select group of people that reside in a convenient geographic location, therefore limiting but validating the attitudes and actions of Christians concerning racial relations within the Christian community. This research assumes that the Christian community needs and wants to identify culturally relevant approaches, historical truths, and theological relevancy to correct or expose false or misunderstood doctrine. At the beginning of this research, I suggested that the focus-group participants and research team members needed to become aware of the complexities that occur with attempts to advance racial reconciliation in a world that prizes division and disunity among races. The rejection of racial reconciliation theology continues to be a debatable issue among Christians. This book seeks to explain the historical and scriptural proof of racial reconciliation as a God-ordained assignment. It is important to me to seek to prove with accuracy the deception of the counter-assumption that racial reconciliation is a myth full of unrealistic expectations. It is my position that the Christian community cannot accomplish its goal of racial unity and harmony among each other without addressing the various deceptive plots to discredit God's sovereignty, intervention, and leadership in the reconciliation process.

DELIMITATIONS

The qualified assumption points toward a social stratification system that rejects all forms of racial equality. It is this hidden agenda and layers of deception that reproduce racial disharmony and defeat meaningful attempts to solve the issues of the racial problems that plague us generation after generation. Historical events prove that past Christian beliefs and behavior patterns still lead to underdiagnosed, unrecognized, and undertreated racial problems.[15] The success of the research depended on the collective attitudes, contributions, and collaboration of all participants. I contend that traditional Christian attitudes toward racial reconciliation are not only socially ineffective and theologically weak, but these unjustifiable convictions are driving the present social conflicts, confusion, and complaints into greater chaos.

Hatred among humans is within the Christian community and the rest of the world. Getting race relations biblically right in this

---

[15] Lee N. June and Sabrina D. Black, *Counseling for Seemingly Impossible Problems: A Biblical Perspective* (Grand Rapids: Zondervan, 2002), 145.

hate-filled world while tension among races is at an all-time high seems to be almost impossible. As mentioned earlier, the emerging Christian attitude has failed to address and appropriate biblically motivated solutions to this racial dilemma adequately. True biblical principles of racial reconciliation will promote the application of unity and ethnic uniqueness; this, however, is offensive to the status quo. The complaints of racial division cater to a lack of accountability on one end and victimology on the opposite end; this is still the demon to defeat.[16] These are limiting and defeating mindsets that paint a compiling census, which undermines actual progress toward biblical racial deepness. The proper plan of surrender among the oppressor and ego-driven institutions and forgiveness from victimization among abused races is the dual detachment (agenda) needed for racial reconciliation success. This challenging approach calls for corporate Christian permission that allows old ways, old behavior patterns, and faulty thinking to be removed from the hearts and actions of all Christians.

MY THESIS STATEMENT

- The desire for ethnic acceptance among all races comes with an enormous price tag that the totality of the Christian community may not be willing to pay. The upside of this challenge is that the Christian community can, and should, lead the way to a higher level of racial unity, not only within the congregation but also in the non-Christian world. The restructuring of stratified programs that indirectly cater to institutionalized and systemic racism becomes the seed for the dismantling and destruction of all forms of racism within the Christian community and the non-Christian

---

[16] Tony Evans, *Oneness Embraced: A Fresh Look at Reconciliation, the Kingdom, and Justice* (Chicago: Moody Publishers, 2011), 21.

world. Furthermore, Christ is the world-changer that now has millions of followers that accept the ministry to "release the oppressed" (Luke 4:18, NIV; Acts 10:38) from bondage. Oppression comes in many forms that can result in economic imbalance, political manipulation, and social deism. Racial injustice and abuse are not suitable for anyone (Proverbs 14:31, 28:3, 28:15–16, 30:14) and should become of no effect on Christianity.

- "He who oppresses the poor reproaches his Maker, but he who honors Him has mercy on the needy" (Proverbs 14:31, NKJV).
- "A poor man who oppresses the poor is like a driving rain which leaves no food" (Proverbs 28:3, NKJV).
- "Like a roaring lion and a charging bear is a wicked ruler over poor people. A ruler who lacks understanding is a great oppressor, but he who hates covetousness will prolong his days" (Proverbs 28:15–16, NKJV).
- "There is a generation whose teeth are like swords, and whose fangs are like knives, to devour the poor from off the earth, and the needy from among men" (Proverbs 30:14, NKJV).

Racial reconciliation is an uncomfortable and demanding task for the Christian community to address and implement. It is a godly plan that requires a righteous biblical approach that can lead to a lasting eternal solution. The need for a Christ-oriented remedy blesses the character of a globally loving God. The daily news, social media platforms, and modern theological debates dictate to the Christian world a universal cry for divine and permanent change. There has been much outstanding research thus far on this topic, which has resulted in many racial barriers being destroyed and cross-culture relationships explored, renewed, and repaired. There are also examples of past events that are tension-packed and confusion-driven that paralyzes sincere attempts to right the wrongs of racism in American Christianity. As a senior pastor, I believe that if our congregation continues to receive accurate teaching and instruction regarding the historical and theological basis for racial reconciliation, then we will have a model with the potential for effective outreach and meaningful relationship-building for all races within the Christian community and the world.

THE DISCUSSION
OF MY THESIS

This section of the book includes a literature review that expands on the data gathered and discussed in the thesis project proposal. It reinforces the thematic information found in the selected literature using paraphrases and footnotes. The theological context and theoretical foundation expanded the subject and application for building relationships that would meet our demand for racial reconciliation, which is a theme that originated in the thesis project proposal.

BLACK CHRISTIAN HISTORY

The theology and history of racial reconciliation resulted in the compilation of historical reports steaming from a variety of historians, scholars, and theologians. There are several startling facts on race relations streaming from research data. According to Carter G. Woodson, every individual has at least two educations, one that has inherited consequences and one that comes with personal education.[17] The implication is that the latter is far more rewarding.

---

[17] Carter G. Woodson, *The Miseducation of the Negro* (Lexington: Tribeca Books, 2016), 86.

The origin of Black people finds its roots in the tenth chapter of Genesis, recorded in the Table of Nations. Scholars agree that this is the oldest ethnographic, historical document that has been found.[18] This biblical text validates the origins of nations and ethnic groups; it also corresponds with the genealogical, geographical, and political data needed to trace the historical roots of ancient Black/African peoples.[19] The Black presence throughout other biblical texts can be validated as well, according to most biblical scholars. There may be different perceptions of skin color among researchers/scholars when investigating the participants identified in the Table of Nations; however, the ancient Hebrew, Greek, and Roman writers mainly agree that ancient Egyptians and Ethiopians were Black and Negroid.[20] A multiethnic background is a highly suggestive conclusion of biblical characters as well. According to J. Daniel Hayes, a non-Caucasian culture context dominated Old and New Testament narratives.[21] Lee June's finding supported a broader rationale and distinction explaining the facts between the origin of Black Christianity and the Black congregation. He wrote, "The biblical Adam and Eve were of African origin (and hence Black), then Blacks were involved directly with God in the beginning."[22] This suggests that Blacks are said to be the main characters in the creation narrative: "And the Lord God formed man of the dust of the ground and breathed into his nostrils the breath of life, and man became a living being" (Genesis 2:7, NKJV). An overwhelming involvement of Blacks in early African Christianity is also documented and supported by many scholars and biblical references (Acts 2:10, 8:26–

---

[18] Walter Arthur McCray, *The Black Presence in the Bible, and the Table of Nations: Genesis 10:1–32* (Chicago: Black Light Fellowship, 1992), 14.

[19] McCray, *Black Presence in the Bible*, 15.

[20] Cain Hope Felder, *Stony the Road We Trod: African American Biblical Interpretation* (Minneapolis: Fortress Press, 1991), 152.

[21] J. Daniel Hayes, *From Every People and Nation: A Biblical Theology of Race* (Downers Grove, Inter Varsity Press, 2003), 45, 141.

[22] Lee June, *Yet with a Steady Beat: The Black Church Through a Psychological and Biblical Lens* (Chicago: Moody Publishers, 2008), 21.

39).[23] The validated reality is that Blacks are the traceable source of human creation and Christianity orientation. It is understood that no scholar can honestly separate these two from each other.[24] Moreover, accepting a multiethnic biblical foundation paves the way for a sound foundation for corrective racial reconciliation theology.

I believe that the biblical Adam and Eve are of the Black race (people of color) of African descent. Scholars such as Walter Arthur McCray and Cain Hope Felder support this history. Lee June concludes, "Then Blacks were involved directly with God from the beginning."[25] The implication is that Blacks are the first originators of God's image, likeness, and history. The kingdom of Cush— or "Cushite," a term representing African people—is mentioned fifty-four times in the Hebrew text of the Old Testament.[26] These Africans lived along the Nile River south of Egypt.[27] When religious individuals falsify or distort the truth, the result is a creation of what June referred to as "a toxic faith system."[28] Acceptance of the involvement of the Black African Kingdom along the Nile south of Egypt in the biblical world must now be accepted and taught. The reason for the correction is based on J. Daniel Hayes's assessment, where he concludes that "many European and American scholars of the nineteenth and early twentieth centuries were blatantly racist."[29] Their doctrine has created an articulated image of God and Blacks that is false and not biblical.

The truth is that Blacks, or people of color, are recognizable in both the Old and New Testaments. The inspired New Testament records that Jesus lived in Egypt for some time as a child (Matthew 2:13–15). Simon of Cyrene helps bear Jesus's cross (Matthew 27:32); on

---

[23] Ibid., 22
[24] Ibid., 21.
[25] June, *Yet with a Steady Beat*, 21.
[26] Hayes, *From Every People and Nation*, 26.
[27] Ibid.
[28] June, *Yet with a Steady Beat*, 144.
[29] Hayes, *From Every People and Nation*, 26.

the day of Pentecost, many African countries represented Christian unity (Acts 2:5–6), and Philip preached Christ to a man of Ethiopian descent (Acts 8:26–39).[30] Some scholars and historians conceptualize a different history connected to Black identity in world history. George Fredrickson, a Stanford historian, interpreted the Black image in the White mind as that of "ape imagery,"[31] and not God imagery. This false imagery contributes to the notion that Blacks are not fully human and that they are considered permanently inferior to the White race.[32] The cost of systematically preserving these layers of deception has cost the Christian community historical shame and enormous embarrassment.

Historical Christianity in America reports the support of racial inequalities through imbalanced educational systems, mass incarceration, segregation, and color-blind politics. Past attempts to correct the wrongs have resulted in deeper damage to race relations.[33] Furthermore, history is somewhat silent, suggesting that there has never been true racial reconciliation between Black and White Christians. Some Christians may believe that authentic racial reconciliation among Blacks and Whites in American Christianity and the world is more of an unrealistic expectation than a reachable phenomenon. And that today's race relations are full of disunity, separation, hatred, and hostility that yet remain among Blacks and Whites. Clarence Shuler's research shows that analytical Blacks do not get enthused about returning to the devastation and degradation that they have experienced; this mindset makes most effort or desire for racial reconciliation undesirable and unwanted.[34] The divisions and prejudices that define the American Christian

[30] June, *Yet with a Steady Beat*, 22.

[31] Jennifer L. Eberhard, *Biased: Uncovering the Hidden Prejudice that Shapes What We See, Think, and Do* (New York: Viking, 2019), 140.

[32] Ibid.

[33] Curtist L. Ivery and Joshua A. Bassett, *America's Urban Crisis, and the Advent of Color-Blind Politics* (New York: Rowman & Littlefield Publishers, 2011), 27.

[34] Clarence Shuler, *Winning the Race to Unity: Is Racial Reconciliation Really Working?* (Chicago: Moody Press, 2003), 141.

community today are real and no longer can afford to be ignored or denied. These injustices await theological correctness, strategic intentionality, and practical creativeness. These historical findings of the origin of Blacks, the deviation of their true identity and legacy, and the various conditions surrounding race relations within the Christian community today are consistent and validated through both old and more recent studies that I have identified in this book.

THEOLOGY

Theology can be a friend or a foe based on the bias and assumption of the leading theologian. Christian theology is a result of a constantly evolving system that recognizes, reorganizes, and recapitalizes the truth concerning God and his Word. Individual scientists suggest that racial inferiority is a product of creation. This theory promotes confusion and conflict among Christians and is not consistent with the biblical account of creation.[35] The subject of racial reconciliation seems trapped in segments of the Christian culture, language, and literature that result in daily scripted behavior and practices among the Christian people.[36] As a modern Yale theologian, Willie James Jennings concludes that a more in-depth investigation of the soil of contemporary theology has grown out of cultural and social clumsiness that is bound by, in the words of Pierre Bourdieu, "the scholastic disposition."[37] Jennings later realized that this deception goes deeper than levels of clumsiness. Still, it is, in his words, "a highly refined process of socialization" that reinforces a complicated system of disassociation and dislocation of information that connects to certain prescribed religious behaviors and attitudes, which enhances, at best,

---

[35] Eberhardt, *Biased*, 137.

[36] Willie James Jennings, *The Christian Imagination: Theology and the Origins of Race* (Ann Arbor: Sheridan Books, 2010), 232.

[37] Ibid., 7.

scholarly theological work.[38] A need for more research on religious bias related to racial reconciliation is apparent. The incorrect perceptions derived from years of destructive theology will continue to plague the racial reconciliation process until corrective theology prevails.

The overall theological premises that cultivate evangelical Christian theology from a historical perspective do point to a process of colonial dominance. Jennings sees these commanding heights of colonial dominance as a painfully superficial reality of the Western Christian church. The results in the form of religion have destroyed the deep desire for real intimacy.[39] Jennings prefers a more biblical way forward, a process that explores the Christian capacity to demonstrate affection through the redemptive work of God's Son in the world.[40] God's gift to the world is reconciliation, but this reconciliation theology cannot be fully grasped or understood until, as Jennings put it, "the deformities of Christian intimacy and identity in modernity" is devalued. When this happens, Christians are now ready to imagine and embrace scriptural reconciliation.[41] On the contrary, some Christian leaders are preaching from the biblical text that racial reconciliation is here and is moving with progressive determination to solve the racial divide among American Christians.

At the 2017 Truth in Conference, hosted by Founders Baptist Church in Spring, Texas, a series of messages was given on the topic of racial unity. The theological insights that provided answers to racial reconciliation and unity within the Christian church and the world validated the assumption that biblical ignorance is the great enemy of racial reconciliation. In one message, H. B. Charles Jr. contended that Jesus destroyed the walls that separated the Jews

[38] Ibid.
[39] Jennings, *The Christian Imagination*, 9.
[40] Ibid.
[41] Ibid., 10.

and the Gentiles through his death on the cross.[42] The authoritative biblical reference is found in Paul's letter to the Ephesians:

> For Christ himself has brought peace to us. He united Jews and Gentiles into one people when in his own body on the cross, he broke down the wall of hostility that separated us. He did this by ending the system of law with its commandments and regulations. He made peace between Jews and Gentiles by creating in himself one new people from the two groups. Together as, Christ reconciled both groups to God by means of his death on the cross, and our hostility toward each other was put to death. He brought this Good News of peace to you gentiles who were far away from him, and peace to the Jews who were near. Now all of us can come to the Father through the same Holy Spirit because of what Christ has done for us. (Ephesians 2:14–18, NLT)

This text reveals that Christ destroyed the barrier and the dividing wall of hostility and has made Jews and Gentile Christians one Body in Christ Jesus.

Juan Sanchez's message explained that the world desires unity and that the miracle of the gospel is not diversity but unified diversity.[43] Racial integration means that Christians are brothers and sisters in Christ (Jew or Gentile) and must function as God's family. Sanchez says the book of Ephesians is God's roadmap to Christian unity, particularly in chapters 4–6, how Paul teaches that individuals of different cultures, languages, tribes and nations

---

[42] H. B. Charles Jr., Danny Akins, Juan Sanchez, Richard Caldwell, Jim Hamilton, Owen Strachan, Carl Hargrove, and Christian George, *A Biblical Answer for Racial Unity* (Woodlands: Kress Biblical Resources, 2017), 38.

[43] Ibid., 57.

are to glorify God with togetherness as Christ's community of believers.[44] The prognosis is that the Christian community in the world should look like the Christian community in the Bible. A good example is found in the second chapter of Acts.

According to Luke, "All the believers devoted themselves to the apostle's teaching, and to fellowship, and to sharing in meals (including the Lord's Supper), and to prayer. A deep sense of awe came over them all, and the apostles performed many miraculous signs and wonders. And all the believers met together in one place and shared everything they had. They sold their property and possessions and shared the money with those in need. They worshipped together at the temple each day, met in homes for the Lord's Supper, and shared their meals with great joy and generosity—all the while praising God and enjoying the goodwill of all the people. And each day the Lord added to their fellowship those who were being saved" (Acts 2:42–47, NLT). Luke describes the infant *ekklesia* as a body of believers manifesting God's living Spirit and dwelling among each other indefatigably.[45] Restoring this biblical version of Christ's community of believers is an ironic causative gesture of hope and love that is further explained in John's writing: "We know how much God loves us, and we have put our trust in his love. God is love, and all who live in love live in God, and God lives in them. And as we live in God, our love grows more perfect. So, we will not be afraid on the day of judgment, but we can face him with confidence because we live like Jesus here in this world" (1 John 4:16–17, NLT). God's love for all humans should manifest itself as a powerful force flowing through the believer to the world.

Danny Akin's message focused on critical principles of what it takes to achieve racial reconciliation and a unified diversity, with Paul's letter to the Philippians as his guiding scripture. Paul wrote,

[44] Charles et al., *Biblical Answer for Racial Unity*, 58.
[45] Lloyd John Ogilvie, *Drumbeat of Love: The Unlimited Power of the Spirit as Revealed in the Book of Acts* (Waco: Word Books, 1980), 31.

- 24 -

"If there is any consolation in Christ, if any comfort of love, if any fellowship of the Spirit, if any affection and mercy, fulfill my joy by being like-minded, having the same love, being of one accord of one mind. Let nothing be done through selfish ambition or conceit, but in lowliness of mind, let each esteem others better than himself. Let each of you look not only for his own interests but also for the interests of others" (Philippians 2:1–4, NKJV).

Akin taught that there are four elements to consider in this text as they relate to racial chemistry among believers: (1) Being of the same mind, (2) having the same love, (3) being in full accord, literally of one soul, and (4) being of one mind.[46] The summation of the message is that the path to racial unity and reconciliation is to have the humble mindset of Christ.[47] Humility is that soulful, childlike disposition of the follower of Christ who is determined to combat negative attitudes toward God's work.

Carl A. Hargrove's presentation reiterates Jennings's preference that a new way must emerge that cultivates genuine racial unity and reconciliation. He reports that from a historical perspective, every continent has demonstrated some form of horrors related to genocide, prejudice, injustice, and systematic oppression.[48] Hargrove's radical solution points to three elements that make up Christian unity. The believers must together believe in a common redemption, a common Redeemer, and a common faith in the one who demonstrated a love based on forgiveness and reconciliation.[49] He made it clear that Christians operating out of progressive compassionate love shall effectively connect, and that this level of unity and hope are not only inevitable but also biblical.

Paul explained to the Romans this personal progression toward corporate oneness: "Therefore, having been justified by faith, we have peace with God through our Lord Jesus Christ, through

---

[46] Charles et al., *Biblical Answer for Racial Unity*, 68.
[47] Ibid., 76.
[48] Ibid., 79.
[49] Ibid., 80.

whom also we have access by faith into this grace in which we stand, and rejoice in hope of the glory of God. And not only that, but we also glory in tribulation, knowing that tribulation produces perseverance and perseverance, character, and character, hope. Now hope does not disappoint, because the love of God has been poured out in our hearts by the Holy Spirit who was given to us" (Romans 5:1–5, NKJV). Notice the words *we, our,* and *us* in this text. In summation, most biblical scholars believe that scriptures are full of pages promoting believers to demonstrate love for God and each other.[50] The summary behind these messages carries a theological mandate for racial reconciliation which is a redemptive love for God and all of his creation.

RECONCILIATION

Wellington Boone denounces the historical sin of slavery in America that was mainly instituted by White Christians. Boone contends that this form of slavery is wrong from a biblical perspective, nor is it God's will. When God's will appears on earth, it must have divine blessedness, with a heavenly promise to validate it. Boone explained that heaven represents all races, kindred, and tongues who worship the King, singing worthy is the Lamb.[51] Therefore, biblical reconciliation starts with God's perfect relationship with humanity. Adam and Eve failed by sinning against God, then God provided the perfect atonement through the death, burial, and resurrection of Jesus Christ, and now humanity's fellowship with God can be restored. This is an explanation for 2 Corinthians 5:17–21, which reveals a spiritual and dynamic union with Christ that is empowered by Christ to establish a ministry of reconciliation

---

[50] Russel D. Moore and Andrew T. Walker, *The Gospel and Racial Reconciliation* (Nashville: B & H Publishing Group, 2016), 47.

[51] Wellington Boone, *Breaking Through: Taking the Kingdom into the Culture by Out-Serving Others* (Nashville: B & H Publishers, 1996), 53.

within the believer's life.[52] This is similar to how Clarence Shuler sees this text (and Ephesians 2:16) as an explanation of spiritual reconciliation but not racial reconciliation.[53] The challenge for modern-day Christianity becomes one of embracing the correct theological perspective and biblical revelation connected to the human/divine experience that explains the relationship breakdown that occurred with God and the builders of the tower of Babel (Genesis 11:1–9). God's reconciliation strategy is to promote a spirit of unity and community through Christ among all races.

Paul explained this Christological reconciliation (I believe it covers both spiritual and racial reconciliation). He wrote,

> If any is in Christ, he is a new creation; the old has gone, the new has come! All this is from God, who reconciled us to himself through Christ and gave us the ministry of reconciliation; that God was reconciling the world to himself in Christ, not counting men's sins against them. And he has committed to us the message of reconciliation. We are therefore Christ's ambassadors, as though God were making his appeal through us. We implore you on Christ's behalf; Be reconcile to God. God made him who had no sin to be sin for us, so that in him we might become the righteousness of God. (2 Corinthians 5:17–21, NIV)

To the Ephesians, Paul wrote,

> For he himself is our peace, who has made the two one and has destroyed the barrier, the dividing wall of hostility, by abolishing in his flesh the law with its commandments and regulations. His purpose

---

[52] Fred Fisher, *Commentary on 1 and 2 Corinthians* (Waco: Word Books, 1977), 343.
[53] Shuler, *Winning the Race to Unity*, 131.

was to create in himself one new man out of the two, thus making peace, and in this one body to reconcile both of them to God through the cross, by which he put to death their hostility. He came and preached peace to you who were far away and peace to those who were near. For through him we both have access to the Father by one Spirit. (Ephesians 2:14–18, NIV)

Reconciliation ministry is about preaching and experiencing salvation to the world based on faith in the redemptive finished work of Christ, not on the requirements of Old Testament law or any other code for human behavior or living.

Moore and Walker understood that what Jesus did on the cross is the religious motivating factor for Christian unity. This is the demonstration of love that God showed humanity by giving his Son as a ransom for all. John wrote, "If we confess our sins, he is faithful and just and will forgive us our sins and purify us from all sin" (1 John 1:9, NIV). This is the loving code for the individual who is motivated to pursue spiritual and racial reconciliation within the context of the Christian community.[54] To reiterate this sentiment, Juan Sanchez believes that the only real genuine agreement is the gospel in action.[55] Evangelical Christian congregations, circles, and organizations prize their ministries on this principle.

Jim Cymbala writes from a pastoral experience of how racial/ spiritual reconciliation can work when God spearheads the process. At Brooklyn Tabernacle church, coming to Christ (or salvation) is offered to and received by all kinds of individuals, such as individuals with addictions, social outcasts, lawyers, businessmen and businesswomen, and bus drivers. Some of the converts are Latinos, African Americans, Caribbean Americans, and Whites. Cymbala sees this as an example of a very diverse assembly that

---

[54] Moore and Walker, *Gospel and Racial Reconciliation*, 41.

[55] Charles et al., *Biblical Answer for Racial Unity*, 47.

the Spirit of God energized and unified supernaturally.[56] Through the worship experiences and the converted individual's testimonies, God's divine love invaded the onlooker's hearts, which resulted in an invitation and acceptance not only of Christ but of each other as one family.[57] Andrea Smith's research corroborates Brooklyn Tabernacle's findings that legislative change is not always needed to mobilize the fight for racial justice; the need boils down to the fact that a change of heart is at the core of solving the race problem in America.[58] The empathetic Christian community seems to be the only exact vehicle that God has ordained to establish unity and intimacy among all races.

One concept called decolonization emerged among Native peoples in 2007. It is a process to undo the process of colonization or to remove any impure colonial thoughts.[59] Smith discredits decolonization as an impossibility. Her position is that global oppression should disappear as leaders build adequate political power that can destroy White supremacist and colonialist privileges within Christian evangelicalism.[60] The fact is that the political machine in America has proven to be very limited when it comes to healing our racial wounds. Therefore, as stated earlier, the desired outcome of multiethnic integration must depend on the empathetic Christian community since history has proven that politics and educational endeavors have fallen short of real restoration and equal coexistence of all races. Also, the felt importance and priority of building godly relationships within the Christian community and the world is the greatest theological hope we should pursue, along with the inevitable task of accomplishing lasting racial harmony.

---

[56] Jim Cymbala, *Fresh Wind, Fresh Fire: What Happens When God's Spirit Invades the Hearts of His People* (Grand Rapids: Zondervan, 2018), 33.

[57] Ibid., 40.

[58] Andrea Smith, *Unreconciled: From Racial Reconciliation to Racial Justice in Christian Evangelicalism* (Durham: Duke University Press, 2019), 57.

[59] Ibid., 197.

[60] Ibid., 198.

BUILDING RELATIONSHIPS

A new identity and relationship with God emerge when salvation occurs in a person's heart. Then new Christian connections arise within the believer's daily life activities. There are Bible verses that explain this new Christological identity and fellowship. This new identity does not exclude a person's racial or ethnic status. This identity is what the Bible calls being "in Christ."[61] God does not eliminate a person's physical or cultural realities when he adopts them into the family of God. It is the new heart that characterizes the new identity. The author of Hebrews wrote,

> This is the covenant I will make with the house of Israel after that time declares the Lord. I will put my laws in their minds and write them on their hearts. I will be their God, and they will be my people. No longer will a man teach his neighbor, or a man his brother, saying "know the Lord," because they will all know me, from the least of them to the greatest. For I will forgive their wickedness and will remember their sins no more. By calling this covenant "new," he has made the first one obsolete; and what is obsolete and aging will soon disappear. (Hebrews 8:10–13, NIV)

This new covenant complements God's authentic conversion for the house of Israel and Gentiles who are grafted into this new arrangement of oneness (Romans 11:17–24; Ephesians 2:11–16). The transition from the old covenant to the new covenant was accomplished through Christ's death and resurrection, and in like fashion when we become one "in Christ." A spiritual dynamic takes

---

[61] Read Genesis 1:26–31 and 2 Corinthians 5:17.

center stage, individually and corporately, and old things give way to new things.

The minister of reconciliation brings to the table an understanding that positive race identity is an uncompromising issue. The author of Psalms 139 wrote, "I praise you because I am fearfully and wonderfully made" (Psalm 139:14, NIV). Anneliese A. Singh suggests that a positive racial identity among all of God's creation is needed when one is confronting an unjust system where one race is inferior to another.[62] A positive race identity means that the individual is secure and accepts personal identity, racial history, and stereotyping.[63] Effective racial relationship building has a lot to do with how Blacks and other victimized minorities respond to microaggressions. Singh explains that microaggressions appear as daily negative messages from a racialized society.[64] These external messages become internal negative stimuli that influence thinking and behavior. Microaggressions are negative racialized communication and reinforcements that deceptively attacks the character or culture of a victimized race.

Shuler maintains that racial relations are not getting better between Blacks and Whites on a larger scale because there is little to no trust among the races.[65] Emerson and Smith surveyed Christians by asking the question, "Do you think that racism is a top priority that Christians should be working to overcome, or not?"[66] Eighty percent of the participants said yes, it should be a top priority. The next question was, "How should racism be addressed?" The answer resulted in four key recommendations to be applied: (1) Try to get to know people of another race, (2) work against discrimination in the job market and the legal system, (3) work to integrate congregations

---

[62] Anneliese A. Singh, *The Racial Healing Handbook* (Oakland: New Harbinger Publications, 2019), 11.

[63] Ibid.

[64] Ibid., 105.

[65] Shuler, *Winning the Race to Unity*, 176.

[66] Michael O. Emerson and Christian Smith, *Divided by Faith* (New York: Oxford University Press, 2000), 120.

racially, and (4) work to incorporate residential neighborhoods racially.[67] These recommendations represent complicated practical solutions and the burden of embracing a theological methodological approach that commands cross-culture communication and social changes. This work is hard and rare.

Craig Garriott believes that Christians must encourage contextual theology, but to do this, Christians must have the power and the discipline to apply the truths that are affirmed. Therefore, the Christian agents for racial unity must understand and accept the facts, mine them, confirm them, and know how to apply them to everyday life.[68] The job of establishing racial justice in a broken world is a hard task that cannot depend on one or two individuals or one or two congregations to accomplish. The world is too broken and divided to put this task on a few faithful Christians, explained Clark and Powell. They believe that every believer can reach out to the least, the last, and the lost to bring divine love and commitment to the entire world.[69] I hope that there are motivational and intentional leaders with strategies that will emerge with the focus of revolutionizing racial relationship-building within the Christian community and the world.

The battleground is within traditional Christian life where attitudes of separateness remain intact and scripturally unchallenged. DeYmaz and Okuwobi give two core commitments that multiethnic congregations and individuals need to incorporate for establishing racial harmony. The Christian congregation needs to welcome people of diverse makeup into significant leadership roles, and critical leadership voices need to intentionally encourage the congregation and community to collaborate toward unity for

---

[67] Ibid., 120.

[68] Doug Serven, *Heal Us, Emmanuel: A Call for Racial Reconciliation, Representation, and Unity in the Church* (Oklahoma City: White Blackbird Books, 2016), 184.

[69] Chap Clark and Kara E. Powell, *Deep Justice in a Broken World: Helping Your Kids Serve Others and Right the Wrongs Around Them* (Grand Rapids: Zondervan, 2007), 242.

kingdom impact.[70] They assume that the relationship-building revolution has already begun and has proven that there are many reachable benefits for the proactive congregation now and in the future.

The informed Black Christian can bring true Christian heritage and identity into an environment, and everyone in that environment benefits from this Black spiritual presence. Molefi Kete Asante recommends that an affirmation of Afrocentricity is needed for Blacks to renew cultural reality.[71] This African identity promotes excellent, provocative, organized, educated, and dependable individuals.[72] Asante believes that the American Black congregation needs a regeneration that will drive the congregation's leadership toward revolutionary social and political consciousness.[73] This challenge in racial reconciliation directives for the Christian community in America is further explained by Haman Cross Jr., of what he called Cross Colors.[74] Haman Cross Jr. challenges the Christian community in America to give a fresh look at racial reconciliation from a different and nontraditional perspective.

This author argues that America's highly racialized society is guilty of an evil that is called partiality. These aggressions, under the umbrella of racism, hinder racial unity and harmony in the Christian community. The hope is that Christians take on this painful and unpopular route of crossing colors by being "reckless"—meaning taking on serious risks to create opportunities for transparent and honest communications with other cultures.[75] The second challenge for the enlightened Christian is to become

---

[70] Mark DeYmaz and Oneya Fennell Okuwobi, *Multiethnic Conversations: An Eight-Week Journey Toward Unity in Your Church* (Indianapolis: Wesleyan Publishing House, 2016), 183.

[71] Molefi Kete Asante, *Afrocentricity* (Trenton: Africa World Press, 1991), 41.

[72] Ibid.

[73] Ibid., 75.

[74] Haman Cross Jr., *Cross Colors: American Christianity in Black and White* (Detroit: Cross Colors with Me, 2015), 138.

[75] Ibid., 139.

"relentless," or have a mindset representing persistent efforts to cross colors.[76] The racial problem, therefore, cannot be approached as a social, philosophical, or secular issue, but as a spiritual one.[77] Haman Cross further validates the historical and theological foundation of erroneous practices that have divided humanity. Most scholars of racial reconciliation agree that the need for improving and implementing racial unity and harmonious relationships within the Christian community can no longer go unchallenged. The fact that race problems continue to plague our communities/ congregations and the wide range of differences on how to address the racial tension in society leaves the Christian with one major question. "What does the Bible say about race (ethnic) relations?"

THEOLOGICAL FOUNDATIONS

The Triune Christian God is a relational being. The composite of the divine existence in reconciliation ministry represents God the Father, God the Son, and God the Holy Spirit. Jesus instructed his disciples to baptize potential believers "in the name of the Father and of the Son and of the Holy Spirit" (Matthew 28:19, NIV). These three Persons of the Godhead share attributes that are preexistent and coequal in quality and essence. The Father, the Word (Logos), and the Spirit work together to create and develop the world as it is known today.[78] John's text communicates that the Trinity enjoys equality and distinction of identity and unity of nature.[79] In the sacred book, everything that the Triune God does and enjoys proves a level of comprehensive cooperation among each divine person. In the creation narrative, God said, "Let us make man in our image,

[76] Ibid., 146.
[77] Cross, *Cross Colors*, 138
[78] Genesis 1:1–2, John 1:1–2.
[79] Merrill C. Tenney, *The Expositor's Bible Commentary: The Gospel of John*, vol. 9, ed. Frank E. Gaebelein (Grand Rapids: Zondervan Publishing House, 1981), 28.

after our likeness."[80] Isaiah 6:8 (NIV) also suggests distinction and unity within the Trinity when the Lord asked, "Whom shall I send, and who will go for us?" This permanent oneness that the Trinity enjoys is always found in Christ.[81] This bonding influence among the Trinity carried over into the relationship that the Creator God developed in the created Adam and Eve and within the Body of Christ.

God expected Adam and Eve not only to enjoy fellowship with the presence of Deity but also with each other. God said, "It is not good for the man to be alone. I will make a helper suitable for him" (Genesis 2:18, NIV). Moses further recorded, "The man said, 'This is now bone of my bones and flesh of my flesh; she shall be called woman, for she was taken out of man. For this reason, a man will leave his father and mother and be united to his wife, and they will become one flesh" (Genesis 2:23–24, NIV).[82] A united, intimate relationship with the Creator God and with his creation describes humanity's foundation for oneness. This premise is suitable for the Christian congregation to develop her role as Christ's bride with the ministry of promoting oneness in her community and society.

The command to the first dwellers of the earth to expand and prosper as synergistic partners is reflective of God's strategy and plan for relational progression (Genesis 1:26–28). The Genesis narrative explains that "God blessed them and said to them, 'Be fruitful and increase in number" (Genesis 1:28a, NIV). This foundational relational principle identifies God's passion for the duplication of a divine model of real unity and harmony among his created first family. It wasn't long before misguided solidarity began to replace God's relational agreement with Adam and Eve. After the fall of the first family, humans continued to increase in number, and the known world learned how to communicate with a high level of godless harmony and togetherness. Moses wrote,

[80]   Genesis 1:26a (KJV).
[81]   John F. Walvoord, *Jesus Christ Our Lord* (Chicago: Moody Press, 1969), 30.
[82]   Genesis 2:18, 2:24, 3:8.

"Now the whole world had one language and a common speech."[83] With this misguided unity that rejected God, an attempt to build a tower to heaven explained the fallen sinful rebellious mindset that sought to make a name for themselves that was independent of God. This tower-building mindset conflicted with God's original plan for a God-centered diverse community.

Brenda Salter McNeil wrote, "Cultural difference and diversity was always a part of God's original plan for human beings."[84] In response to this conflict of interest, God complicated their ability to communicate with each other, thus scattering them and destroying their tower-building plan.

Keil and Delitzsch explain the tower builder's failure to follow God's original intent: "For, according to the divine purpose, men were to fill the earth, *i.e.*, to spread over the whole earth, not indeed to separate, but to maintain their inward unity notwithstanding their dispersion."[85] Therefore, God confused the language. "The Lord said, "If as one people speaking the same language, they have begun to do this, then nothing they plan to do will be impossible for them. Come, let us go down and confuse their language so they will not understand each other" (Genesis 11:7, NIV). This swift execution of the Trinitarian decree resolved differences in ethnic groups, families, and languages according to Candlish.[86] God's long-term focus, after the Tower of Babel's intervention, was to build a better intimate relationship with all of humanity.

Abram was that promised link that would result in the expansion of God's original intent to develop divine friendships, diverse relationships, and global blessings with God and all families

---

[83] Genesis 11:1 (NIV).

[84] Brenda Salter McNeil, *Roadmap to Reconciliation 2.0* (Downers Grove: IVP, 2015), 28.

[85] C. F. Keil and F. Delitzsch, *Commentary on the Old Testament: The Pentateuch* vol. 1 (Peabody: Hendrickson Publishers, 1989), 173.

[86] Robert S. Candlish, *Studies in Genesis* (Grand Rapids: Kregel Publications, 1979), 176.

of the earth (Genesis 12:1–3). According to James, "the scripture was fulfilled that says,

'Abraham believed God, and it was credited to him as righteousness, and he was called God's friend'" (James 2:23, NIV).[87] That desire to be in a relationship with God the Father is the void that reconciliation ministers seek to fill in a person's life. Just like Abraham, we too must believe in God and declare righteousness through his word. The full manifestation of this restored relationship of God with humanity comes through believing and receiving the incarnate Christ as Lord and Savior of our lives. Divine grace adopts us and places us as dear children in our spiritual family of God. John recorded, "He was in the world, and though the world was made through him, the world did not recognize him. He came to that which was his own, but his own did not receive him. Yet to all who received him, to those who believed in his name, he gave the right to become children of God" (John 1:10–12, NIV). Barnes suggests that people who receive Christ are united with the Lord Jesus and are regarded as children of the Highest.[88] This divine election complements the relational position that the believer has with Jesus Christ our Redeemer. We also learn a Christian principle that nothing should separate us from this loving relationship with the Father through Christ,[89] resulting in a noticeable attitude of respect and reverence for God and all of his creation. That's why Paul asked, "Who shall separate us from the love of Christ?" (Romans 8:35, NIV).[90] God invites the world to be the recipients of this restored relationship (John 3:16) and, ultimately, a representation of his divine redemptive love (2 Corinthians 5:20). This makes the reconciliation message

---

[87] See Genesis 12:1–3, James 2:23.
[88] Albert Barnes, *Notes on the New Testament: Explanatory and Practical, Luke and John* (Grand Rapids: Baker Book House, 1957), 179.
[89] Romans 8:35.
[90] Kenneth Boa, *Conformed to His Image: Biblical and Practical Approaches to Spiritual Formation* (Grand Rapids: Zondervan, 2001), 207.

concerning Jesus Christ the greatest mission for his community of believers, to communicate love and forgiveness in all languages of the world.

The core of racial reconciliation theology comes with the abandonment of spiritual death that separated God from humanity and the revival of spiritual life that places the believer back into union with God and others. This restoration process enhances a methodology of spiritual and physical interactions with the Creator and his creation that overcomes hate and evilness in a way that brings glory to God and oneness to all creation. Paul explained the process this way: "And we, who with unveiled faces all reflect the Lord's glory, are being transformed into his likeness with ever-increasing glory, which comes from the Lord, who is the Spirit" (2 Corinthians 3:18, NIV).[91] Individuals from every nation have the invitation to be reconciled first to God and second to God's creation through Jesus Christ. Being "in Christ" produces a radical change in the believer's life, actions, and behavior patterns.[92] Putting off the old sinful nature and replacing it with Christ's life, the new nature, which depowers sin and empowers righteousness in the believer's life. Without this radical transformation of the individual, reconciliation between God and man is artificial and ineffective. God's new creative work in the believer is described as a new life of devotion to Christ with new attitudes and actions.[93] The weakening and replacement of the sinful nature in the believer will determine the outward effects of the indwelling life of Christ that impacts the believer's thinking, conduct, and lifestyle. This inward transformation is needed first before the contagious work to build loving relationships in the Christian community and the world is manifested.

---

[91] 2 Corinthians 3:18 and 5:17 (NIV).

[92] David E. Garland, *The New American Commentary: An Exegetical and Theological Exposition of the Holy Scriptures, 2 Corinthians* vol. 29 (Nashville: B & H Publishing, 1999), 286.

[93] John F. Walvoord and Roy B. Zuck, *The Bible Knowledge Commentary: New Testament* (USA: Victor Books, 1989), 568.

PRINCIPLES TO BUILDING RELATIONSHIPS

Divine relationship building is accomplished through principles and examples that can be taken directly from God's Word. This research suggests that six principles are needed for racial reconciliation theology to accomplish its fullest desire. The first principle in the relationship-building process is an acknowledgment of faith in the Triune God and the Word of God. This principle is foundational for spiritual reconciliation and social trustworthiness. The complexities of combining the theology of the universal Christian God within the physical world are to be realized and applied before any form of biblical reconciliation can be manifested. Faith in God creates the capability of the believing individual to reunite in a relationship with God and to embrace all of God's creation through a new set of lenses. This move of faith (total belief and trust in the message of reconciliation, which is the gospel of Jesus Christ) connects individuals with the family of God and his kingdom.

Jesus informed Nicodemus, "No one can see the kingdom of God unless he is born again" (John 3:3, NIV). The problem of disconnect and disunity with God must be solved before an acceptable union with others is approved by God. Paul's letter to the Ephesians explains the validity of saving faith: "For it is by grace you have been saved, through faith-and this not from yourselves, it is the gift of God-not by works, so that no one can boast. For we are God's workmanship, created in Christ Jesus to do good works, which God prepared in advance for us to do" (Ephesians 2:8–10, NIV). Paul recognized his apostolic assignment to build godly relationships in the world through the preaching of the gospel: "I am obligated both to Greeks and non-Greeks, both to the wise and the foolish. That is why I am so eager to preach the gospel also to you who are at Rome. I am not ashamed of the gospel, because it is the power of God for the salvation of everyone who believes; first for the Jew, then for the Gentile. For in the gospel a righteousness from God is revealed, a righteousness that is by faith from first to last, just as it is written: The righteous will live by faith" (Romans 1:14–17, NIV). Belief in the gospel message is the beginning of the pursuit and practice of building new and lasting relationships with God and others.

The second principle in the relationship-building process is fellowship with God and others. This step compels believers to spend quality time with God, with one another, and with potential believers. The Greek word is *koinonia*. This element binds the Christian community together with commonality, companionship, and comradeship. It is a mutual partnership at work through participation in the divine nature.[94] It is God's design plan filled with all the fullness of God.[95] It is the outward evidence that the world needs to see so they can be motivated to embrace real Christian fellowship. According to John's writing, "This is the message we have heard from him and declare to you; God is light; in him, there is no darkness at all. If we claim to have fellowship with him yet walk in the darkness, we lie and do not live by the truth. But if we walk in the light, as he is in the light, we have fellowship with one another, and the blood of Jesus, his Son, purifies us from all sin" (1

[94] Geoffrey W. Bromiley, *Theological Dictionary of the New Testament* (Grand Rapids: William B. Eerdmans Publishing Company, 1985), 449.
[95] Eric L. Johnson, *God and Soul Care: The Therapeutic Resources of the Christian Faith* (Downers Grove: IVP Academic, 2017), 554.

John 1:5, NIV). The greatest quality of light is that it exposes the correct nature of things.

The opposite of Christian fellowship is destructive contention. Proverbs 21:9 (AMP) warns the people of God, "It is better to dwell in a corner of the housetop [on the flat oriental roof, exposed to all kinds of weather] than in a house shared with a nagging, quarrelsome and faultfinding woman." This woman represents anyone who cannot (or will not) pursue a peaceful and loving environment.[96] The example of fellowship that God endorses among humans represents first Trinitarian unity, family unity, and unity gained through the promulgation of the gospel (Matthew 5:14–16). As mentioned earlier, the root of human fellowship started with Adam and Eve. When Adam saw Eve for the first time, Adam declared, that Eve is "bone of my bones and flesh from my flesh. This one is called woman, for from man was taken this one." Therefore "a man leaves his father and his mother and clings to his wife, and they become one flesh" (Genesis 2:23–24, TLV). The desire for intimate fellowship grows among believers and others as Christ's identity (Light to the world) is recognized and applauded in the congregation and the community we serve.

Effective fellowship with each other is crucial for the advancement of the relationship between the reconciler and the reconciled. God enjoyed and sought fellowship with Adam and Eve in the garden of Eden (Genesis 3:8). Jesus summoned the twelve disciples to be united with him before doing ministry together (Matthew 10:1). Paul emphasized in his writings the importance of the Christian calling in the fellowship with the Son, Jesus Christ the Lord, and with the Holy Spirit: "God, who has called you into fellowship with his Son Jesus Christ our Lord, is faithful" (1 Corinthians 1:9, NIV). Paul also wrote to the Corinthians, "May the grace of the Lord Jesus Christ, and the love of God, and the fellowship of the Holy Spirit be with you all" (2 Corinthians 13:14,

---

[96] Charles Bridges, *A Modern Study in the Book of Proverbs* (Milford: Mott Media, 1978), 441.

NIV). The Psalmist wrote, "Behold, how good and how pleasant it is for brethren to dwell together in unity!" (Psalm 133:1, AMP). This fellowship mandate with Christ and each other is not temporary but eternal. Paul wrote, "The Lord himself will come down from heaven, with a loud command, with the voice of the archangel and with the trumpet call of God, and the dead in Christ will rise first, after that, we who are still alive and left will be caught up together with them in the clouds to meet the Lord in the air. And so we will be with the Lord forever" (1 Thessalonians 4:16–17, NIV). According to this scripture, a reunion of all Christians with Christ is an end-time event. This cumulated level of unity and fellowship with God and among his believers is considered to be a lifestyle blessed by God now and throughout eternity. Oneness is the divine aim and goal of Christian fellowship. It requires the Father and the Son to spend quality time with the loving believer through the Spirit of God (John 14:23, 17:21; 1 John 1:3). Therefore, true Christian fellowship demonstrates an inseparable love and mutual respect among God's elects.

The third principle in the relationship-building process is friendship with God and with others. This principle promotes divine love for others in the congregation and the community. Christian friendships are mainly built around the believer's godly ability to deeply care for the well-being of others. A friend is visible in times of crisis and turmoil (Genesis 38:12). A true friend always shows compassion and support and will be around in times of adversity. One of the authors of Proverbs wrote, "A friend is always loyal, and a brother is born to help in time of need" (Proverbs 17:17, NLT). This text also suggests that this level of friendship has no exceptions or mitigating circumstances.[97] Biblical wisdom teaches that true friendship is a priceless commodity. "Oil and perfume rejoice the heart; so, does the sweetness of a friend's counsel that comes from the heart"

[97] David A. Hubbard, *The Communicator's Commentary: Proverbs* (Dallas: Word Books, 1989), 264.

(Proverbs 27:9, AMP). "Iron sharpens iron; so, a man sharpens the countenance of his friend [to show rage or worthy purpose]" (Proverbs 27:17, AMP). Moses and Abraham (great faithful leaders) were called friends of God (Exodus 33:2; 2 Chronicles 20:7). True Christian friendship is not automatic but demands loving evolutionary Christological measures.[98] Another proverb suggests, "A man with many friends may be harmed by them, but there is a friend who sticks closer than a brother" (Proverbs 18:24, TLV). Jesus informed his disciples, "My command is this: Love each other as I have loved you. Greater love has no one than this, that he lay down his life for his friends. You are my friends if you do what I command" (John 15:12–14, NIV). I believe that cross-cultured friendships are the anchors that secure Christ's ministry of reconciliation and provide hope for his vision of Christian unity that is yet to be fully developed.

In this step, a shift in positional responsibility and accountability in the relationship is developed. Jesus went on to declare, "I no longer call you servants, because a servant does not know his master's business. Instead, I have called you friends, for everything that I have learned from my Father I have made known to you" (John 15:15, NIV). The God-ordained relationship progresses from slaves to friends to brothers (Romans 8:14–17, Galatians 3:27–4:8) according to Stern.[99] The reconciliation minister sees the dismantling of the notion of an inferiority/superiority relationship resolved and replaced with deeper empathy and intimacy for each other. Jesus informed the disciples that their relationships have grown and matured to a level that accommodates a clearer vision and revelation of the Father's heart for companionship.

---

[98] Merrill C. Tenney, *The Expositor's Bible Commentary: The Gospel of John* vol. 9 (Grand Rapids: Zondervan, 1981), 153.
[99] David H. Stern, *Jewish New Testament Commentary* (Clarksville: Jewish New Testament Publication Inc., 1992), 201.

The fourth principle in the relationship-building process is the public recognition of the multicultural spiritual dynamic of the Christian family. This principle explains who is entrusted with the Father's will and that there is a definite diversity among those chosen children of God. The gospels reported that Jesus was initially rejected by his Jewish people but later accepted by both Jewish and non-Jewish people. Jesus came to his people of cultural relevance but was initially rejected. Yet all individuals who received the Jewish Son of God as the Messiah were placed in the family of God. John wrote, "He came to that which was his own, but his own did not receive him. Yet to all who received him, to those who believed, he gave the right to become children of God-children born not of natural descent, nor of human decision or a husband's will, but born of God" (John 1:11–13, NIV). When Jesus was informed of the presence of his biological family members, his response reiterated this divine alignment and prioritization of individuals who belong in the household of God. Jesus asked, "Who is my mother, and who are my brothers? Pointing to the disciples, Jesus said, "Here are my mother and my brothers. For whoever does the will of my Father in heaven is my brother and sister and mother" (Matthew 12:48–50, NIV).

The nearest and dearest relations connected to Jesus are individuals who may not have kindred ties but those who are sustained toward him.[100] This alignment in the family of God produces righteous divisions. Jesus's message is clear: "Do not think that I have come to bring peace upon the earth; I have not come to bring peace but a sword. And a man's foes will be they of his own household" (Matthew 10:34, 10:36, AMP). God's Christian family, according to the Bible, is made up of Jewish and Gentile believers who may not belong to the same bloodline but share the same spiritual purpose and DNA.

---

[100] Barnes, *Notes on the New Testament*, 137.

The fifth principle in the relationship-building process is the intentionality and obligation of the Christian community to demonstrate forgiveness of past sins that hindered racial unity and supported an anti-multiethnic agenda. This principle seeks to correct and heal individuals and races of people of past hurts, faults, failures, and sins. This principle also calls for the individual believer's commitment to combat all future forms of racial disunity in the Body of Christ and the world. Forgiveness is a necessity in the grace age; it is the correct response to spiritual restoration (Galatians 6:1) and divine pardon.[101] Paul's advice to the Ephesians states, "Get rid of all bitterness, rage, anger, harsh words, and slander, as well as all types of evil behavior. Instead, be kind to each other, tenderhearted, forgiving one another, just as God through Christ has forgiven you" (Ephesians 4:31–32, NLT). Biblical forgiveness seals the deal for effective spiritual and racial reconciliation in the Christian community and the world.

The final principle in the relationship-building process is the reception of God's favor (grace) in the relationships enjoyed by proactive Christians. This final principle explains God's reaction to biblical reconciliation. God's favor complements God's people as persecuted but blessed influential individuals in the world. A narrative in the book of Acts explains this concept. Luke wrote, "And the multitude of them that believed were of one heart and one soul: neither said any of them that ought of the things which he possessed was his own; but they had all things common. And with great power gave the apostles witness of the resurrection of the Lord Jesus: and great grace was upon them all" (Acts 4:32–33, KJV). In this text, the physically persecuted followers of Christ demonstrated oneness in spirit, affection, emotion, understanding, intelligence, and thought. In response, favor with God and man

---

[101] Lewis Sperry Chafer, *Systematic Theology: Doctrinal Summarization* Vol. 7 (Dallas: Dallas Seminary Press, 1976), 165.

prevailed.[102] The unfolding of God's plan for the believer and the Christian community is to show that true alignment with Christ justifies and glorifies the minister of reconciliation with Christ's sovereign grace.[103] Because of the disciple's corporate collaboration and their absence of selfishness, these followers of Christ in this text were recipients of religious persecution as well as divine blessedness.

---

[102] W. Robertson Nicoll, *The Expositor's Greek Testament* vol. 2 (Grand Rapids: William B. Eerdmans Publishing company, 1990), 137.

[103] Steven J. Lawson, *Foundations of Grace: A Long Line of Godly Men* vol. 1 (Orlando: Reformation Trust Publishing, 2006), 19.

THEORETICAL
FOUNDATIONS

The *Evangelical Dictionary of Theology* defines racism as follows:

> A learned belief in racial superiority, which
> includes the belief that race determines
> intellectual, cultural, and moral capacities. The
> practice of racism includes both racial prejudice
> and discrimination against others based on their
> race or ethnicity. Two primary forms of racism,
> individual and institutional, are generally viewed
> as products of either psychological or social forces.
> Racism in any form is a sin that embodies both
> moral and spiritual dimensions.[104]

Building on this definition, June asserts that the Christian
community has the potential to be the "healing community" that
can meet the needs of those affected by institutional racism.[105]
Shuler sees the need for the church to update racial reconciliation
as a principle to be explored before meaningful and cross-cultural

---

[104] Walter A. Elwell, *Evangelical Dictionary of Theology* 2nd ed. (Grand Rapids: Baker
Book House Company, 2001), 978.
[105] June, *Yet with a Steady Beat*, 115.

relationships can come to fruition.[106] The most relevant approach to racial healing that accommodates the aims of this book is the given emphasis on Bible-based truths that correlate with the notion that brotherly love must continue within the Christian community as an active force and a call to action, which will combat problematic racial degenerative issues. As the Hebrew writer puts it, "Keep on loving each other as brothers and sisters" (Hebrews 13:1, NLT).

The advent of racial reconciliation and building cross-cultural communication within the Christian community has approached many crossroads with various concepts and approaches to choose from. One approach deals with the examination of history as a predictor of what the future entails. Clarence Shuler suggests that there are four reasons why African American Christians are not motivated to pursue racial reconciliation: (1) White Christians do not care about the plight of the Black community; (2) African Americans see racial reconciliation as a form of Europeanization; (3) African Americans fear losing the last institution that is owned and controlled by Blacks, the local church; and (4) racism is still a reality within and outside of the Black church.[107] This overwhelming focus on historical resentment distracts from the biblical achievement of racial reconciliation.

Tony Evans suggests that "the core problem of racial disunity in America is the failure to understand and execute a kingdom-based theology on both righteousness and justice."[108] The significant challenge for a pure kingdom approach resides in the notion that all Christians representing all ethnic groups are prone to embrace, accept, and abide by the biblical implications of racial reconciliation. This level of racial reconciliation is yet to manifest itself.

According to Hays, racial reconciliation is already a reality because God's people are categorically made up of multiethnic

---

[106] Shuler, *Winning the Race to Unity*, 144.

[107] Shuler, *Winning the Race to Unity*, 141–143.

[108] Tony Evans, *Oneness Embraced: A Fresh Look at Reconciliation, the Kingdom, and Justice* (Chicago: Moody Publishers, 2011), 22.

assemblies representing all tribes, languages, peoples, and nations to create a worship atmosphere that focuses on God's throne.[109] The combination of kingdom living and racial allyship has the potential to impact biblical guidelines for the engagement of healthy confrontation of racial discrimination and oppression.[110] This therapeutic approach has proven that focus groups that are designed to address racial issues have a "healthy effect" of making the group participants realize their ethnocentric assumptions and limiting beliefs.[111] Focus-group experiences have resulted in group collusion that can dictate what level of open discussion, critical thinking, and problem-solving techniques can be used.[112] The more diversified the group is, the greater the chances of racial awareness, and feelings are deemed to be expressed.[113] However, deficient socialization, destructive church practices, and past failed attempts at racial harmonization have hindered the actualization of racial dialogue for racial equality.[114] With that said, all is not lost, many Christians today realize the need to continue to pursue true racial reconciliation directives and ministries.

The gap between expectations and experiences is important to this study. The model for this study allows the participants to determine both the level of biblical communication needed and the creative application of the biblical knowledge gained and applied for the improvement of race relations. The desired outcome of the study suggests a practical and effective agenda that the participants agree to adopt as an improved policy for cross-culture and diversity success within the religious community.

---

[109] J. Daniel Hayes, *From Every People and Nation: A Biblical Theology of Race* (Downers Grove, Inter Varsity Press, 2003), 205.

[110] Anneliese A. Singh, *The Racial Healing Handbook* (Oakland: New Harbinger Publications, 2019), 173.

[111] Samuel T. Gladding, *Groups: A Counseling Specialty* 7th ed. (New York: Pearson, 2016), 129.

[112] Ibid.

[113] Ibid.

[114] Hayes, *From Every People and Nation*, 206.

The model further suggests that all Christians demonstrate love practically, continuously, and foundationally as a prescribed way of life.[115] Church practices that are below biblical expectations lead to greater confusion and divisions that do not represent the founder of the Christian community, Jesus Christ (Matthew 16:18). Paul rebuked the Corinthians because of divisions in the congregation. Paul wrote, "I appeal to you, brothers, in the name of our Lord Jesus Christ, that all of you agree with one another so that there may be no divisions among you and that you may be perfectly united in mind and thought" (1 Corinthians 1:10, NIV). An intentional dialogue aimed at uniting interfaith group thinking that attacks anti-Christological love remains the solid therapeutic path to keep pursuing and expanding.

The applied approach that focuses on getting to know people of other ethnic groups is called the friendship-ology theory.[116] This approach, authored by a non-Black congregation, has the potential to be positive, with limited counterproductive challenges. I suggest a combination of the friendship-ology theory connected with proper historical, psychological, and theological initiatives in a ministry context among all Christians. This represents a deeper, more realistic approach to building, repairing, and restoring race relations within the Christian community and the world.

According to Grudem, the key to race redemption is to embrace restoration and reconciliation. Restoration demands that the offender conform to the right behavior from destructive and unrighteous behavior patterns, and reconciliation challenges all parties to demonstrate a united righteous front with God and each other.[117] Therefore, from a Christian therapeutic perspective, racial

---

[115] George H. Guthrie, *Hebrews: The NIV Application Commentary, From Biblical Text to Contemporary Life.* (Grand Rapids: Zondervan, 1998), 435.

[116] Michael O. Emerson and Christian Smith, *Divided by Faith* (New York: Oxford University Press, 2000), 123.

[117] Wayne Grudem, *Systematic Theology: An Introduction to Biblical Doctrine* (Grand Rapids: Zondervan, 2000), 894.

reconciliation's core motive and purpose is church discipline.[118] It is how God replaces the enmity and hostility between him and humanity with peace and fellowship with him and the human race.[119]

Reconciliation ministry challenges the Christian community to speak out and stand against the social evil of favoritism and to demonstrate Christian love and compassion toward both believers and nonbelievers.[120] This moral perspective within the Christian community is the practical and theological approach to racial healing and the authentic concept of racial unity.

---

[118] Ibid.

[119] Paul Enns, *The Moody Handbook of Theology* (Chicago: Moody Publishers, 2008), 244.

[120] Millard J. Erickson, *Christian Theology* 2nd ed. (Grand Rapids: Baker Academic, 2009), 1067.

MY METHODOLOGY

Building Better Relationships (BBR) is a six-session, biblically tailored racial reconciliation program that focuses on teaching and helping Christian congregations and organizations to improve cross-cultural relations with the hope of destroying racism within and without our known world. BBR expands on the friendship-ology theory with a spiritual-discipline perspective resulting in corrective ecclesiology. This approach is to teach a variety of scriptural truths that establishes a biblical foundation validating assumptions for corrective racial reconciliation theology. Consistent with our Bible study focus-group learning patterns, building blocks activate the influencing factors (e.g., participant motivation, individual ownership, and decision-making prerogatives). Each BBR session consisted of the focus-group facilitator (the senior pastor) introducing one of the racial reconciliation principles for textual observation, discussion, and dialogue. The concluding session of BBR accommodated the participants' fellowship, brainstorming, and plan of action to eradicate racism within our Christian community, resulting in new and improved race reconciliation policies.

INTERVENTION DESIGN

Racial reconciliation is a journey that is talked about at great lengths with increasing frustration and desperation among most

American Christians today. The desire to heal and prevent higher racial division within our congregation and American Christianity was the primary foundation for the thesis proposal project. The process toward a successful solution began with identifying the roots connected to the problem of racial discord and disunity among us. It is the position of the thesis problem that there is a limit or lack of theological knowledge of racial reconciliation within our congregation and the Christian community, and by teaching the Christian community what the Bible reveals concerning the history of racial reconciliation, then corrective socialization becomes achievable. Biblical history shows the attitudes and actions of characters who enforced the need for racial healing. A case study of spiritual and political disharmony manifested itself when Jesus announced that he had to go through Samaria (John 4:4). According to the narrative, the history among the Jews and Samaritans had become systematically disharmonious. "Jews refuse to have anything to do with Samaritans" (John 4:9, NLT). With a more in-depth education and study of biblical history, this biblical text solidly reveals the problems of biased worship agendas, race stereotyping, and traditional religious behavior patterns that were socially destructive and are prevalent within our world today.

The research plan to implement racial reconciliation training within our congregation as a model for others was the heartbeat of the research. The research project had three phases:

First, a thirty-minute interview was designed to gather data from ten (five from each church) consenting leaders of Lord of Lords Ministries in Detroit, Michigan, a Black congregation, and leaders of His Church Anglican, a non-Black congregation in Detroit's suburb. The interviews gathered data concerning the level of biblical understanding and indebtedness of the subject matter within the two groups. This first phase paved the way for phase two.

The second phase was to teach a six-session Bible study on multiethnic conversations and collaboration. This study prepared the focus group's participants for the application of how to reconcile and fellowship with other races and diverse ethnic groups. The discussion agenda topics were as follows:

1. Why multiethnic?
2. Why now?
3. Obstacles to date
4. Systemic issues
5. What God is doing
6. How should I respond?
7. How should the church respond?
8. Living a multiethnic Christian life

The meeting place for the six-session training was at Lord of Lords Ministries and on social media platforms on Wednesdays from 6:30 p.m. to 7:30 p.m. for six weeks. The final phase began once the participants of the training received their six-session foundational teaching and instructions on expanding our congregations' racial reconciliation programs. In the final phase, the participants also focused on advancing the reconciliation ministry regionally. Through brainstorming and strategic planning, a challenge for the implementation of building better relationships (BBR) locally and worldwide surfaced. The desire to keep learning, teaching, and researching how to develop healthy and loving relationships among all individuals became our core motivation to keep going forward. Other results from our brainstorming sessions included the development of a congregational policy for effective cross-cultural integration and experiences. Our Bible study material became a guideline (possibly one day a workbook) for an in-depth study of theology-based principles to help build cross-cultural relationships that will help heal a divided world. The development of a regional support group of senior pastors and leaders was also a result of our brainstorming sessions.

The ages of survey participants and program stakeholders were at least eighteen years of age. The educational level was limited to individuals earning up to a master's degree. Recruitment of an equal number of male and female participants established concern for balanced perspectives (we had six females and five males). A support group of local interfaith leaders was added to the research after the six-week training for their deeper understanding and regional implementation of the recommended model. These leaders are meeting monthly for training and fellowship. The interview and the data-gathering stage were to compile information. The teaching phase was to obtain enough information on racism's historical development so that the formation of true racial identity could be reestablished, and the argument to remove the inaccurate genealogical posting from our theology could be accomplished. It is the accuracy of scriptural interpretation and the cumulative historical data that moved me and the focus groups from recognizing the problems of racism and racial disconnections to a solution that will alleviate these problems or fill a gap in the pursuit of reducing the social problems in our world.

What made this subject of racial reconciliation so viable for me (and within our focus-group discussions) is the reality that a Black man named George Floyd died because a White police officer held his knee on George's neck for eight minutes and forty-six seconds. The global response to George Floyd's death (and other similar deaths of minorities) and the rise in hate crimes in our nation exposed the painful reality that there are perspectives among the religious communities that are anti-God. These responses exposed a variety of attitudes toward racial injustices that have no biblical foundation but justify the force behind the dysfunctional socialization we experience in America and the world. The other conclusion that I had drawn was that the Christian community lacked effective solutions to the race problems that plagued their congregations and neighborhoods. George Floyd's death, along with other disturbing news that was seen all over the world, exposed America's racism, its depth, and its impact on American soil and around the world. Racial reconciliation and racial healing are in the hands, and now the hearts, of the faith community. The various marches, protests, and outcries are evidence that not only is racial healing needed but also wanted by most people representing all races.

Another assumption of the study is that racial injustice is one of the most talked-about subjects on social media outlets today. Politicians have promised to eradicate the problem, social groups meet daily to strategize solutions to the problem, and spiritual leaders are praying constantly to ask God for solutions to the problem. All of this points to one solid moral conclusion that there is a desperate desire to attack the problem of racism with the determination to remove racial disharmony and disconnect from the face of the earth and to bring the global community to a successful procedure that will replace social division with multiethnic unity. It is my hope and the research team's optimism that racial disconnect is seen as a solvable problem. The focus for the solution of the racial problem incorporates historical and theological correctness as a therapeutic approach that recommends the application of biblical principles and spiritual disciplines as a practical agenda for all people of faith to implore.

Biblical doctrine and end-time prophecy on racial issues help us to understand the current and future challenges that confront the religious community. Jesus informed his audience that the end-time events would include hatred among nations and a limited level of love among his followers (read Matthew 24:1–14). The believer of Jesus Christ has been strategically placed on earth by Christ to combat and transform disconnected love among earth dwellers into divine redemptive love. This love reconciles us to God's purpose and grace. Paul wrote to the Romans, "God demonstrates his own love for us in this: while we were still sinners, Christ died for us. Since we have now been justified by his blood, how much more shall we be saved from God's wrath through him! For if, when we were God's enemies, we were reconciled to him through the death of his Son, how much more, having been reconciled, shall we be saved through his life! Not only is this so, but we also rejoice in

God through our Lord Jesus Christ, through whom we have now received reconciliation" (Romans 5:8–11, NIV).

This love is the primary foundation for the religious community (1 Corinthians 13:1–13). It is Christ's desired priority (Revelations 2:4) and the remedy for sustained Christian unity (Hebrews 13:1). Recently, 560 cities marched in protest of the racial disparity portrayed among Americans in one day. The high level of disregard and disrespect against minorities has reached its boiling point, and the call for all believers of Jesus Christ to demonstrate divine love, respect, and equality for everyone seems to be the right solution.

IMPLEMENTATION OF THE
INTERVENTION DESIGN

A Zoom meeting with the Greater Detroit Partnership on June 10, 2020, gave the project an indirect beginning and a head start into the process. A group of twelve Christian leaders, mainly senior pastors (seven Black and five non-Black leaders), participated in the meeting. The theme for a discussion focused on strategies that addressed the racial disharmony and discouragement in the world and the Christian community that went public after the death of George Floyd. The desire for a greater understanding of multiethnic relations and racial healing from a theological perspective furthered the conversation beyond this Zoom meeting. My thesis project in that meeting became my passion and motivation to understand and address our regional and environmental structured racism. My thesis project gained congregational acceptance and corporate momentum as I launched my project intentions. At the start of this project, many local leaders agreed with me that a level of ignorance and impatience clouded past attempts toward regional racial reconciliation and that the desire for more research and understanding of racial reconciliation prevailed.

In the Zoom meeting, it was suggested that I identify interested senior pastors and ministers in the region who were interested in implementing a racial reconciliation teaching platform within their area of influence. The model that the leaders will use will represent the strategies understood from the recommendations and documented experiences identified in the research. The senior pastors and ministers, the interviewees, and the project stakeholders shared with me their thoughts and focus on how to make a social impact using the raw material retrieved from them and to use the pertinent data gathered for project advancement. Once the results of the survey were in, the pastoral leaders identified the curriculum for the post-interview training. The final phase of the project dealt with all participants coming together with the regional leaders for fellowship, dialogue, implementation, and expansion of the corporate strategy toward racial reconciliation programming in our region.

The primary open-ended questions in the survey for the focus group's participants were as follows:

- Why are churches not involved in racial reconciliation programs? If there are churches with racial reconciliation programs, give your personal thoughts about the church's plans.
- What are your personal feelings about race relations within the Christian community, America, and the world?
- What are the reasons that most Christian churches are not multiethnic?
- How can building relationships with other races become a church priority?
- What scriptures relate to racial reconciliation in the Bible?
- What are the barriers to racial reconciliation within the Christian community, America, and the world?
- Are there additional personal concerns and comments concerning racial reconciliation?

The answers to the primary questions compiled and organized by the research team assisted me, as the group's facilitator, in making directional recommendations and sharing meaningful conversations to share for deeper relationship development.

The estimated timeline to accomplish the training process was six weeks. The first week consisted of explaining the teaching process to the focus-group participants for the introduction of material, mutual commitment, consent, and directives. The second week entailed biblical teaching on race and ethnic history, development, and identity from a biblical perspective. The student's involvement, input, and help in the organization of thoughts, perceptions, and feelings through the teaching and conversations determined the level of engagement needed for individual, congregational, and social change. The oversight of the data gathering and teaching was the responsibility of the senior pastor/facilitator of the focus group.

The third and fourth sessions covered more combined teaching and discussion on scripture references, personal experiences, race relations, and multiethnic conversations from assigned literature: Taylor Cox Jr.'s *Creating Positive Race Relations: What You Can Do to Make a Difference* (Author Solutions, 2020) and Mark DeYmaz and Oneya Fennell Okuwobi's *Multiethnic Conversations: An Eight-Week Journey toward Unity in Your Church* (2016).

The fifth session consisted of examining crucial selected teaching on particular Bible-based relationship-building processes led by the group's facilitator.[121]

The sixth-session activities focused on post-questionnaires, mutual fellowship, corporate brainstorming, and the agreement on intentional implementations of how to achieve racial unity and harmony within our congregation and the communities we serve.

---

[121] See appendix B.

RESEARCH RESULTS

The findings derived from the research came from recorded interviews, congregational leaders' surveys, and questionnaires from focus-group participants. A total of ten participants volunteered and were selected for the research while other volunteers were selected to work on various aspects of the research project. A discovery for me was witnessing the characterization formation of the participants as they emerged and became model leaders of the ministry of reconciliation. The interviews revealed the degree of knowledge needed to convey greater understanding and motives behind the low level of racial reconciliation portrayed within our congregation and region. It also gave me the data for the project that was crucial for research progression and implementation.

In our first post-training fellowship with the local pastors and leaders and project participants, we found that 60 percent of all pastors invited were reluctant to involve their congregation members in the research project for fear of the unknown. Out of the fellowship participants (70 percent non-Black and 30 percent Black), leaders showed optimism and excitement to have their ministries address racial reconciliation as a God-ordained task. There was a high level of optimism, enthusiasm, and joy among everyone at this gathering. This level of righteous sensitivity encouraged these leaders of different religious affiliations and ethnic identities to move forward for greater success in racial reconciliation.

The interviews and meetings established individual assessments that confirmed biases and deep-seated racism that was either inherited learned behavior patterns or faulty culturally empowered thinking. My main focus was on the congregation I pastor, Lord of Lords Ministries. I am indebted to my friends Domenic Morelli (Faith Works) and Pastor Allen Kannapell (His Church Anglican) and Brent Hansen for their valuable support, contributions, and interviews. Pastor Allen and I selected five leaders from our congregations to help us understand and facilitate this racial reconciliation project. My overwhelming desire, emerging from the data collected, was to develop an agenda that fostered learning from Bible principles as they relate to race relations and how God defines ethnic unity. My collaboration with the interviewee's thoughts and survey results determined in my assessment the urgent need for a shift from investigation to the application of a more meaningful racial reconciliation ministry for the Christian community. A recommendation for embracing the data as a guidepost for building and developing multiethnic relationships emerged from our group discussions. It became obvious that biblical ignorance and scholarly misconceptions relating to reconciliation ministry in biblical narratives were good reasons to continue the journey. Furthermore, I concur that there is a high level of individuals in this world with good intentions to eliminate the racial disconnect but they lack categorically sufficient knowledge and motivation to do what needs to be done.

The project's purpose was addressed and the solvability of the project's problem was understood and successfully debated among the research participants for the implementation of a model for our congregational use. This research concludes that meaningful effective teaching and training are needed to combat racial disharmony within the faith community and the world. I believe that there are greater truths that will emerge from studying racial reconciliation, from deeper theological research, hermeneutical perspectives, and healthy collaborative dialogues. Most of the assumptions from this research are consistent with already-established premises and patterns of problematic racial thinking and behavior among Christians. I now see more Christians embodying a level of truth revealed to them through God's Word that may be controversial but God-driven. This truth behind Christian unity must be communicated by the reconciliation minister to others with a clear vision, compassionate love for all humans, and dutiful courage. This call for the radical transformation of the Christian community is gaining momentum as a shared ministry with eternal accountability.

MY SUMMARY OF
INTERVIEWS

THEME: A TABOO SUBJECT

Our congregation has a history of involvement in racial reconciliation programs with other local congregations and institutions. My first interview was with one of our evolving leaders of biblical racial reconciliation. She has helped us organize outreach programs where our congregation and suburban congregations teamed up together to provide inner-city communities with food, clothing, and toys. Her understanding is that people tend to stay away from racial reconciliation ministry because dealing with the diversity of races creates racial tension that relates to a bigger issue in America. Unfortunately, not many individuals dare to deal with race issues even within their homes and community.

She is a single mother with two daughters ages thirteen and seventeen. She works a full-time job and holds a bachelor's degree in psychology. And she is passionate about her children living in a world that judges them based on their character and not the color of their skin. With her renewed interest in racial reconciliation came certain troubling topics that we discussed, which lead to the main topic of our interview, which I called tabooism.

Our conversation exposed the burden of holistic freedom

that many minorities only dream about. The reason for the divisions among races in America and the religious community is impostorism. This makes racial reconciliation a taboo subject to some people. The reality of slavery, Jim Crow laws, and many other modern race-related problems defining America's Christianity continue to create this taboo notion. We both agreed that spiritual and secular leaders have struggled with implementing programs to build positive race relations within our communities and the world. Her observation is that many individuals feel that pursuing racial harmony is a vain imagination. She feels that certain race-related agendas are franchised for the greedy business sector, which makes it almost impossible to remove them from society. She is correct that outside of Christ's mission to save souls and change hearts, there is no real solution for human unity. Keep in mind, Jesus did not separate or scatter people purposefully for profit or greed. He instructed his followers to go into all the nations to talk to all people and bring them into a place of spiritual oneness.

There are misguided Christians who believe that the soul winner's job is hard and unrealistic. They prefer to focus on the development of Jesus's character formed in the believer because internal transformation is more important to them than any external religious conformity. It is our observation that this kind of thinking carries a social venom that has the potential to destroy the Christian community. She addressed what I call a distorted view of Christianity, where Christian leaders and churchgoers are detouring from a reconciliation campaign because of tainted convictions related to who qualifies to be reconciled with God and each other. My understanding is that everybody should be able to live free from all forms of bondage. Through Christ's blood, all humans can be delivered from economic, social, mental, and spiritual slavery. This freedom helps the children of God to not entangle their thoughts and actions on faulty osmosis (Philippians 4:8) but effortlessly observe to do everything that's written in God's Word (Joshua 1:8), and then the needed outcome is accomplished.

The position of breaking bad habits of division and establishing good habits for unity cannot be underestimated. Why don't we see a radical change to solve racial problems? Why do Christians speak and promote division? Can Christian harmony be manifested before Christ's return? These are questions I was challenged with during the interview. The reality of this taboo mindset is unfortunate because most divisions among Christians are not endorsed by the Bible. They are based on preconceived unbiblical learned behavior. The explanation for the divine/human division is reported in scripture (Genesis 3:20–24, 11:1–9). This judgment is ingrained in the human experience as a result of fallen humanity. It will take theistic thought and action to restore unity with God and among humans. This is the biblical concept of unity called the Body of Christ. If our thinking is influenced by Christ's redemptive work, then we will behave privately and publicly according to God's standards and not man's opinions.

The reality of ignorance or denial of racial disconnect continues to divide and devastate our world. The major question that emerged from our conversation is, how can God's people have unity if no one wants to face those racial issues that are dividing us? The biblical fact is that the believer has the authority to overcome anything that is not endorsed by God (Luke 10:19). As children of the Light, we are called to expose and reprove the darkness of this world (Ephesians 5:10–14); therefore, it is crucial that we shed more light (knowledge) on racial disunity and how to conquer it.

It is easier not to talk about or demonstrate racial reconciliation in our assemblies, so we tend to go the simpler route of traditional tolerance. As a congregational leader, I don't want my parishioners to stop coming to our worship services; therefore, I tend to avoid topics that are messy and controversial to our well-established inoffensive weekly agenda. This agenda is based on current culturally relevant issues and concerns. I am comfortable communicating within my specific ethnic group. I am knowledgeable and familiar with my culture, and I know and relate to my congregation's pain and joys.

As their human shepherd, I can relate to their wants and needs; and because I want to be their successful pastor, my focus is on their individual needs. There is nothing wrong with connecting with people through corporate familiarity. The problem occurs when the pastor and the congregation have limited vision and refuse to move from witnessing in their Jerusalem to their Judea, Samaria, and the ends of the earth, which is Christ's agenda.

Learning to include unfamiliarity (different approaches to ministry) with my established denominational norms is one of my leadership flaws. I don't think that I am the only leader who struggles with this problem. This research assumption is that more Christian leaders are challenging themselves and their congregations to accommodate the needs of other ethnic and religious groups by including options in styles of worship, teaching, and preaching to bring a greater awareness of God's kingdom into our places of worship. The challenge for me is to take the unpopular route of embracing cultural diversity in hopes of cultivating worshippers who can come together to worship the Father in spirit and truth without compromising the fundamentals of the Christian faith.

The key to effective racial reconciliation leadership training is to focus on how a leader should love all people unconditionally. This calls for self-growth and ministry exposure, which will be accepted by some and rejected by others. Leadership engagement questions are as follows: Will all leaders connect with all races? Is it important for Christians to know who the other races of people are? What are their ethnic likes and dislikes? How do you study other races to correctly reach out and minister to them? These important questions need to be addressed to abolish this concept of taboo thinking. Reconciliation wisdom implies that Christians should know or learn how other cultures think, feel, and live.

There must be a real value in cultural engagement. There is value in questions such as the following: Where do people like to work? What do people like to eat? These are relevant questions for the racial reconciliation minister. The minister should first know people before attempting to convert people into Christ's followers. What are people's values, fears, and inspirations? It was Jesus who said, "Where your treasure is there your heart will be also" (Luke 12:34, KJV). What perspectives and priorities do people focus on? When correct understanding, boldness, and confidence evade the reconciliation minister's thinking, then outreach to other cultures can be manageable.

Jesus purposely went to Samaria. He no longer wanted to ignore those people of Samaria or the divisions between the Jews and Samaritans. Let me identify two biblical nuggets that are helping me to overcome unbiblical cultural prohibitions: The first is from Jesus's conversation with the Samaritan woman that our worship of God should be in unity in spirit and truth (John 4:23). The truth may take us out of our traditional forms of worship into genuine and pure interaction with spirit in the spirit realm. Another is found in chapter 10 of Acts, in which Peter had a dream where God came to him in this dream and told him to eat certain foods. Peter thought the food was unclean based on Jewish teaching, so he rejected the food. Three times the Lord informed Peter that no one can rightly say that the food (creation) that God had blessed was unclean. God told Peter to go preach the gospel to non-Jews so that the truth and love of God will resonate in the Gentiles' hearts (read Acts 10:9–48). The lesson taught to Peter in this text is that God promotes unity among Jews and Gentiles regardless of their traditional eating habits. The more we focus on God and his word, the more likely we can be unified even though there are differences in the way we worship and the food we eat.

The core biblical principle of this interview is to embrace the truth that God loves the world—meaning God loves all people. The Bible did not say that God so loved Black people or God so loved White people or Asian people, etc. God loves the human race so much that he gave Jesus to all of us. He is the only begotten Son of God. If we believe in Christ our Redeemer, we will receive everlasting life and demonstrate unconditional love for all humans with no other conditions to be met (John 3:16). The burden or pain that's connected to this research is that the message of reconciliation, which includes racial unity, is very seldom preached, taught, and practiced in our society. The Bible refers to people based on their spirituality, nationality, or ethnic makeup, but very seldom is the color of someone's skin mentioned.

There are two barriers to or strongholds for racial reconciliation in our modern world that should not be ignored: the evilness connected to present-day politics and major unforgiveness between races. For those reasons, racial reconciliation ministry should be taken on by the Christian community as an urgent spiritual solution to our racial problem. Prophetically, everything is coming to a filtered climax, and the challenge for the people of God is to stand up and speak courageously about changing racial disconnections to racial unity. If we don't, our society will become more anti-Bible. The challenge given to the reader of this book is to take a bold stand and declare that racial disconnect is not right at any time and any place.

I also believe that the individual who can make the greatest impact when it comes to racial healing is the bold anointed reconciliation minister who has conquered the spirit of fear and replaced such fear with faith in God and his Word. This is the good fight of faith that triumphs over human obstacles, religious gimmicks, and spiritual wickedness. The kingdom ambassador knows that he/she is already ordained to fight and win. The kingdom ambassador is on the front line of warfare ministry, demonstrating God's love by pulling down strongholds of human disconnect and disunity on this earth.

Another challenge in this book is to convince the passive believer to become aggressive and fall in line with fighting the sin of racism. It is too dangerous to remain silent concerning racial reconciliation. Racial harmony and Christian oneness have to be addressed now as a vital solution to our deteriorating influence. God's power, God's presence, and God's Spirit must invigorate each believer and make them the change agents that this world needs. Our procrastination has caught up with us, and we cannot afford to lose any more relevance in a world that already doubts our legitimacy.

THEME: PROGRESSIVE PAIN

My second interviewee is a first-year college student. She opened her interview with the understanding and acknowledgment that our congregation is one of a few ministries that seek to promote racial reconciliation programs in our region. She mentioned how she enjoys our fellowships with non-Black congregations. The horrible reality for her is that the previous congregations she has been part of, especially in their summer Bible classes and summer vacation Bible school, did not focus on anything racial, but they had the representation of different ethnic groups in their congregations. She believes that racial reconciliation has to be more than just teaching about race relations—it must be about faith in action, applying the Word of God to help build quality relationships with all of humanity. Her concern is how all congregations will get training to implement racial reconciliation programs and how the Christian community will bring all races together for meaningful interaction. She believes that this is important for the resurgence of American Christianity because it is taught in the Word of God that the Body of Christ should build each other up and promote unity within our faith (Ephesians 4:3). It would be awesome if Christians could peacefully talk to each other about race issues. Why? Because God created every ethnic group with peculiar cultural differences, creative abilities, and unique ideals that all humans can benefit from; but she feels that human diversity has been manipulated and misunderstood by anti-God agendas. The culmination of experiences and knowledge about how different cultures function can help the Christian community to connect rightly and positively for the good of the entire world.

Our college student expressed a level of confusion and disappointment because she believes that not too many Americans are looking to understand the different cultural norms and ethnic perspectives in society. Her belief is based on the fact that only a few individuals in the past sought sacrificially to solve the racial issues in this world and were limited in their success. She expressed her thoughts on race relations with teary eyes identifying her wounded heart. Because of her emotional brokenness, I limited our dialogue. I realized that it was a difficult task for her to talk about and articulate fully some of her racial experiences. Her biggest wound turned out to be an indictment against the older Christian community. She felt that they (we) have not valued biblical unity as a priority or done enough to secure real racial change for the younger Christians. The older Christians, in her opinion, have not fully addressed past failures, concerns, and strategies for the implementation of racial harmony as a paved road toward success for the next generation of leaders. I agreed with her that there are indeed hurtful realities and devastating histories explaining the dysfunction of American Christianity. These issues have to be filtered correctly for our younger generation. The embarrassing past of racial disunity among Christians doesn't sit well with this young Christian visionary and many of her peers. They are disturbed because most of the Christian community is too segregated and still sanctions this ungodly behavior of racism.

She argued that many individuals don't want to come together and confront race problems, mainly because of their conditioned negativity and their inability to release to God people and issues that need healing and closure. Let me pause to say our ignorance, our arrogance, lack of responsibility, and our denial of our history have resulted in unnecessary shame, injustice, and discrimination for our younger generation to deal with. There is still too much hatred and racial disparity in our Christian nation and within our Christian community. This interview has awakened me to another reality: They (Christian youth) expect their older Christian leaders to come together, talk openly, and correct the racial problems of the past so their future will bring greater truth and glory to the Body of Christ. The refusal to prioritize racial problems and differences and talk openly about the racial disparity that exists complicates the goal of community bonding, and it discourages multiethnic initiatives among our youth. If we are going to inspire our youth to take ownership of racial reconciliation ministry, we must demonstrate to them a strong commitment to God's Word, an improved affirmation of the Christian faith, and a simple proven process to unite all ethnic groups as a model to be duplicated.

Effective racial reconciliation programs must focus on generational needs, cultural differences, and future conversions. These programs should help us to see that there are God-established bridges that can connect disconnected people of all ages. Our focus is to help young Christians to gain understanding and truth about the race problems in our world. However, we cannot stop there. We must lead them through their emotional roller coasters, deep-seated biases, and unconscious symbolism so they can overcome both personal and corporate racism.

I constantly ask myself, why do I challenge our youth to promote Christian unity as a godly standard when they see very little unity among Christian leadership today? The harsh reality is that many Christians feel that reconciliation ministry is not their purpose in life and that fighting/solving racial problems is advocacy work for skilled and trained individuals. We cannot afford to continue to neglect the hurt and pain of our youth that's derived from racial problems. We must honestly teach them how systemic ills still influence our present-day thinking and behavior. The remedy is teaching God's perspective and passion for repairing relationships and, most importantly, how to create a loving atmosphere for the healing of all damaged emotions. Racial reconciliation is a very important subject for the next generation of Christians to address because there seem to be older Christians in the pews that are mean-spirited and closed-minded. This mindset has hindered the corporate consciousness needed for God's young people to move forward as a united force for change.

THEME: THE APPLICATION OF GOD'S WORD

I was challenged by the next interviewee—an elder of our congregation who believes that most Christians are not mature enough in God's Word to implement the ministry of racial reconciliation in their homes and their communities. In this interview, we talked about a noticeable weakness in our congregation and the Christian community: it is the lack of biblical understanding of how to promote unity among all of God's creations in this world. I teach our reconciliation team that they must have a desire for a reconciliation ministry, along with an understanding that there is a divine connection between spiritual unity and ethnic representation. The reconciliation leader's focus is evangelistic training coupled with Christ's cross-culture instructions found in the Great Commission (Matthew 28:16–20). Many Christians don't understand that winning souls for Christ is a form of warfare. Keep in mind that the reconciliation minister has the support of scripture to implore spiritual weapons of war that will help implement Christ's strategic planning and implementation of this soul-winning ministry (read 2 Corinthians 10:3–5 and 1 Corinthians 2:6–10).

My position as the senior pastor is, in many ways, the lead racial reconciliation minister of our congregation because I am the one that normally gauges the spiritual and social climate of the membership, and I'm one of the spiritual stakeholders of our community. The question is, can we teach and demonstrate God's Word to the congregation in a way that establishes biblical principles for real racial reconciliation programming in our area? I agree with my interviewee that our congregation and community need biblical motivation and corporate maturity to implement love and forgiveness for all opposition that rejects God's plan for unity.

Why is there a lack of unconditional love among God's people for all people? Why is it so hard to find compassion and empathy in this world? Where are loyalty and concern for the well-being of all citizens? This God-like mentality of loving one another in the Christian community is not seen enough. The indictment is that many Christians today distance themselves from those who are rejected, suffering hardships, or are wrongly persecuted. Christians are instructed to be a blessing to the world, especially to each other. Paul wrote, "As we have opportunity, let us do good to all people, especially to those who belong to the family of believers" (Galatians 6:10, NIV). It is advantageous to live according to the Bible, which instructs us to be a favor-connector to all peoples. Many individuals in my race (African Americans) and other races suffer from undeserved pain and agony steaming from unresolved slavery innuendos and misunderstood apologies. This has resulted in a high level of mistrust and fear among Christians. The implication is that deep-seated denial and biblical ignorance can stagnate the progress of racial reconciliation. It can hold the believer back from moving forward with positive, progressive biblical stimuli.

In the Bible, we found keys to explain racial reconciliation directives. Jesus compared the job of catching fish to the ministry of reconciliation (Mark 1:16–18). His disciples are considered fishers of humans; they have been instructed by Christ to launch out into the deep waters (where a variety of fish reside) to catch a variety and abundance of fish (individuals). Jesus also knew that his disciples would experience a great harvest of souls but the work would be overwhelming because of a lack of ministers (Luke 10:2). A reconciliation campaign that challenges the Christian to overcome all barriers and pursue various kinds of people with working faith (James 2:26, KJV) is in harmony with Jesus's instruction to pray to the "Lord of the Harvest" for the increase of ministers (Luke 10:2). Racial reconciliation methodology can gain momentum when our working faith is not mediocre, our love for the world is God's love, and our prayers are effective (James 5:16).

The major key for reconciliation ministry is effective prayer, it enhances the Christian worker's spiritual growth, challenges proactiveness, and encourages and maintains spiritual unity through peace and truth (Ephesians 4:3, 4:15). Effective prayer and Bible study challenge Christians to live in harmony and covenant agreement with each other (Ecclesiastes 4:9–12). We have to agree with one another based on God's standards and not on man-made ideologies. When we lose sight of God's Word, or if the truth of his Word is not reiterated regularly from the pulpit and in our homes, alternative standards for living replace biblical instructions.

A scripture that was repeatedly referenced in the interview was from the seventh chapter of the Second Chronicles, which says, "If My people who are called by My name, will humble themselves, and pray, and seek My face, and turn from their wicked ways; then will I hear from heaven, and will forgive their sin, and heal their land" (2 Chronicles 7:14, NKJV). In this text, a timeless principle is stated. God is requesting repentance from his people so he can provide restoration and healing. Repentance for restoration is also found in the New Testament. Paul wrote, "Brothers, If someone is caught in a sin, you who are spiritual should restore him gently" (Galatians 6:1, NIV). John wrote, "If we confess our sins, he is faithful and just and will forgive us our sins and purify us from all unrighteousness" (1 John 1:9, NIV). God's Word also teaches that every individual must repent (have a change of heart) to secure their redemption (a one-time act of faith in the gospel of the kingdom, Acts 2:38) and to be restored from practicing sin. The twofold reconciliation plan is for every believer to receive the grace of God through redemptive repentance and restoration repentance.

God's plan will not change; everyone gets an opportunity to be saved, and no believer will be condemned (John 3:17, Romans 8:1). The overabundance of God's blessings and the healing of our land will be manifested when the doers of God's Word become the influencers in all parts of God's world. A major barrier that hinders racial reconciliation within the Christian community is fear of change. This fear does not come from God (2 Timothy 1:7). This barrier to racial reconciliation focuses on the inability of the believer to yield to the God-given spirit of love, power, and soundness of thought. The understanding of this text inspired me to build better racial communication based on replacing all fear with faith in God and his Word.

The Word of God is the divine dialogue between God and his creation. This research has helped me to understand that there are well-meaning Christians who have misinterpreted the Word of God when it comes to the application of racial reconciliation ministry. This misinformation, or a lack of an in-depth study of the reconciliation ministry, has resulted in spiritual deafness or blindness identified in some believers and has created, in Paul's words, "the spirit of bondage" (Romans 8:15, KJV). There are no mistakes in God or his Word—the mistakes are in humanity's inability to align themselves with the truth revealed in God's Word.

The effective minister of God always seeks God's direction (Romans 8:14), meditates daily on God's teaching (Psalm 1:2), and practices God's Word for true individual and social impact (James 1:22). We as God's spiritual children have to love the Word and digest the Word so that his instructions come off the page and rest in our hearts for holy living. God's Word is hidden in the believer's heart, and it does not allow Satan to come in and dictate their behavior (Psalm 119:11). The Word-empowered believer can take the wisdom and instructions of God and destroy any barrier built by evildoers. Everything that a believer does is scrutinized by the unbelieving world; therefore, everything that the unbelieving world does should be explained to the believer by God. Whatever the believer signs on to should always reflect the mind, heart, and nature of God. We concluded the interview with the understanding that the key to implementing racial reconciliation in our society is to mimic Christ's attitude and thinking as a lifestyle. It is the daily renewing of the believer's thinking through meditation on scripture that brings individual and community transformation into conformity with God's will, which is his Word.

THEME: THE PROBLEM OF FEAR

Fear is a negative force that hinders racial reconciliation. In my next interview with one of our outreach ministers, her conversation led to the assumption that the Christian community is prideful, angry, ignorant, faithless, fearful, and influenced by antichrist-stereotyped images. God wants Christians to come together for reconciliation, but the fear of failure has crippled significant past efforts. Can the Christian leader demonstrate personal boldness that embraces the reconciliation ministry? Can we see each other as brothers and sisters in God's family? Why are we overly concerned with skin color and cultural differences? How do we destroy the fear of cross-culture evangelism? Where and when can strategic reconciliation theology occur? The House of Worship is the home for assembling the believers. The desired outcome is believers coming together in a place where everyone can be family regardless of how they look. No relationship should be based on fear or being afraid of someone because of false stereotypes. Christians must learn to give each person a chance to promote and declare true brotherhood or sisterhood in the Lord. This demands true empathy with conscious transparency. This brings us to the reality of being in Christ and Christ in us. This radical change of identity in the Christian community becomes the new normal.

Christ's work on the cross is our example and motive for reconciliation ministry. If the Christian can overcome this fear of failure in reconciliation ministry, the reward will be a combination of God's presence and power pervading the world through the believer. God anoints his ministers with confidence to possess the land for his glory. He will always position his people for kingdom advancement. The vision of a diverse righteous people that represent God's kingdom, where the recipients share mutual authority, should be a top priority for the reconciliation ambassador.

Kingdom authority among us is the weapon that shuts the enemy of racial disconnect down. Keep in mind that the problems associated with dysfunctional race relations within the Christian community and in the world are bigger than any local assembly. This global revelation of racial reconciliation is now flowing into our thinking, inspiring our spirits, and prioritizing our activities to redefine civility. There are individuals all over the world that have embraced with courage a multiethnic God-centered society. These agents of change must be willing to destroy all barriers that seclude us or hinder us from corporate oneness.

We must be led by God's Spirit to collaborate with other cultures in the world as ministers of reconciliation, encouraging people of every nation to experience different worship styles and spiritual practices that may be different from our normality. This intentionality takes wisdom, courage, and boldness. Some of the questions that emerged from this interview are as follows: Do we have evangelism boldness? Do we have the boldness to ask someone of another ethnic group to come and see how we worship at our House of Worship?

I believe that the reconciliation ministers must be willing to travel outside their confront zones and go into unfamiliar territories and communities. These are sacrifices that every change agent will have to make. Through prayer and meditation, the Holy Spirit will empower, lead, and guide the minister to areas that should be evangelized. With the combination of confidence and training, the minister can cross cultures and make new friends. The reassuring thought is that before the foundation of the world, God has established his redemptive plan (Ephesians 1:4–5) in the believer's heart to build his community on this earth.

The challenge for today's Christians is that each one of us should destroy selfish traditions that disinvite diverse people to our worship experience and services and should have meaningful activities with them even though they may do things a little differently than us. I can say that there is an increase in the recruitment and the establishment of a new kind of spiritual leader that represents strength, bravery, and fearlessness for biblical change. This attribute of Christlikeness is foundational for the racial reconciliation ministry. Christ demonstrated publicly how God loves all of his human creations and how he wants to redeem them back to him through the blood of Jesus Christ. John wrote, "For God so loved the world that he gave His only begotten Son, that whoever believes in Him should not perish, but have everlasting life" (John 3:16, NKJV). This scripture implies that Jesus did not have hate or fear when he sacrificed his life on the cross. Hate is the opposite of love, and fear is the opposite of faith. We, as God's agents for change accept this reconciliation ministry knowing that we must abandon the spirit of fear and overcome all hateful attitudes that have hindered progress in the past so that we no longer will be deceived or paralyzed by selfish, fearful, and evil motives against anyone.

THEME: THE PROBLEM OF IGNORANCE

Not too many congregations are involved in racial reconciliation programs because of an unawareness of the magnitude of the racial problems in the world. They either don't know or are in denial of past documented racial bigotry, race-related disagreements, and misrepresentation of the truth. This interview with one of our outreach ministers set the stage for the conversation on how difficult it is to implement racial reconciliation as a Bible-mandated ministry. This situation of bringing all races together is a big and troubling problem and has been going on for too many years that it seems to some individuals an impossible problem to solve. From this research, I have learned that many Christians don't want to deal with racial reconciliation ministry because it will open up old painful wounds. People feel that they will get a lot of backlash from individuals that are against racial unity. Many people that proclaim the Christian faith are against mixing different races because they were taught to either degrade or fear certain people. This makes it hard for the reconciliation minister to promote oneness as a theological concept, thus creating a tense environment. Another concern that was discussed in our interview was that reconciliation ministry programs have the potential to hinder the tithes and offerings of the big supporters that don't want racial unity in their congregation.

These barriers suggest that there is a high level of ignorance, selfishness, and misinformation concerning racial reconciliation among most Christian congregations. Our congregation has tried to reeducate and motivate our membership to learn more about implementing racial reconciliation programs that we believe are needed and effective. We may not change into a multiethnic congregation, but we believe that at some level, we can have positive, loving relationships with all peoples, including other cultures and congregations of this world. In my research on racial unity and congregational life, I have learned a valuable lesson that racial reconciliation (God-approved relationships among races) is a good process for building solid, healthy relationships throughout the world. I see racial reconciliation as something good because it brings out our capacity to practice the love of God among each other and in the community. This practical approach to racial reconciliation theology reiterates the belief that all humans come from one human race through one loving Father God who loves his creation through his incarnate Son. Standing on the revelation that we are Christ's *ekklesia* (community) transforming this world for God's glory is priceless. This knowledge that God is the Father of all creation and we are his redeemed ambassadors should help us to regulate the divine plan of the cohabitation and the redemption of all humans in this place called earth.

THEME: THE FATHERHOOD OF GOD

A major topic of reconciliation theology that concerned every interviewee was the Fatherhood of God. All humans are progenitors of the Heavenly Father according to the Bible. As believers, we are his image-bearers, first by creation (Genesis 1:26, Jeremiah 32:27) and second by redemption (Colossians. 3:9–10, John 1:12). Let me explain: In the creation narrative, God breathed into Adam's nostrils the breath of life, and Adam became a functional God-like living human being (Genesis 2:7; Acts 17:25). Paul says that God's fatherhood is in heaven and on the earth (Ephesians 3:15). The author of Hebrews calls him the "Father of our spirits" (Hebrews 12:9, NIV). James identified him as the "Father of the heavenly lights" (James 1:17, NIV). The book of Job and Genesis called the angels "the sons of God" (Job 1:6, 2:1; Genesis 6:4, KJV). It is very important for every human being to know his/her connection with the Creator/Father of all creation (Malachi 2:10, Acts 17:28). Paul declared that "there is but one God, the Father, from whom all things came and for whom we live; and there is but one Lord, Jesus Christ, through whom we live. But not everyone knows this" (1 Corinthians 6–7, NIV). This truth that all humans (fallen or redeemed) are children of God does not sit well with all people.

Throughout the Bible, we learn about the love, mercy, and intimacy of the Father for his entire universe. He says, "Israel is my firstborn son" (Exodus 4:22, NIV). Nathan prophesied to David concerning God's love for David which affected Solomon. He said, "I will be his father, and he will be my son" (2 Samuel 7:14, NIV). The Psalmist reiterated this sentiment when he wrote, "As a father has compassion on his children, so the Lord has compassion on those who fear him; for he knows how we are formed, he remembers that we are dust" (Psalms 103:13–14, NIV). The Father challenges his children to seek his full intimacy: "Come out from among them and be separate, touch no unclean thing, and I will receive you. I will be a Father to you, and you will be my sons and daughters" (2 Corinthians 6:17–18, NIV). David explained his closeness with the Father when he wrote, "You formed my inward parts; you covered me in my mother's womb. I will praise you, for I am fearfully and wonderfully made; marvelous are your works, and that my soul knows very well" (Psalms 139:13–14, NIV). Believers are enlightened once they understand that they are adopted into the family of God (Romans 8:14–17) and are being formed into the image of Christ (Galatians 4:19), but we also must accept that God the Father has a unique filiation with all humans in a physical as well as a spiritual capacity.

One way to fight social and cultural division and advance the ministry of reconciliation is to become a lover of all people. My dad was a people person; he did not mind being around and learning from different kinds of people with different cultural norms. He would purposefully create events and activities that brought different cultures together for learning, engagement, and collaboration. Our tent revivals are reflective of his mentoring. This fatherly attitude has helped me to know that there are unique traits in all people waiting to be accepted, applauded, and appreciated. This fatherly attitude cannot be afraid to destroy negative animosities that divide people and replace them with healthy curiosities that connect different ethnic groups. I stated earlier that racial reconciliation is a good thing. That Christians should be okay with it. That love is the divine force that is demonstrated through the believer to the world. Accepting the reality that there are a lot of ignorant people in the world who are deceived in thought that leads to racist behavior and that they don't see the need to change helps the child of God to keep advocating for real reconciliation ministry. Keep in mind that all religious leaders' intentions and motives do not come from the loving Father of the universe. According to Jesus, the unbeliever's father is the Devil (John 8:44), and their thoughts and behavior are wicked and contrary to God's thoughts and ways (Isaiah 55:8–9); therefore, these individuals that are influenced by the Devil need to be restored to the original relationship that humans had with God the Father.

The absence of the Father's love for all of his creation is mainly portrayed in individuals who don't believe in God's plan of redemption for universal collaboration and cohabitation. This is still a major problem in the Christian community. This age-old conflict calls for the Christian community to move with intellectual and spiritual responsibility. The world needs ministers who can demonstrate godly favor that embraces racial harmony as a mission mandate. Unbelievers, babes in Christ, and some older Christians need to be taught to duplicate the ways of the Father and how he unconditionally loves all people. This research is helping me to see that I need a personal attitude adjustment. That I have not completely accepted and understood some of my biased cultural, political, and religious thoughts that are anti-Bible. I now feel the pressure and pain that this ministry exposes, as it addresses my (our) need for deeper training in racial reconciliation.

Keep in mind that ignorant people are not always evil people but may have been exposed to the wrong education or information. I represent people who have been taught with limitations the biblical perspective of ethnic unity. Our minds need to be renewed for a deeper understanding of the importance of Christ's family in the community. Mind renewal and transformed thinking are necessary for healing prayer and proper mentorship (discipleship). The challenge is to reeducate ourselves on the subject of demonstrating fatherly love to wounded family members (Luke 15:11–31). This should be a high priority because the essence of Christ's passionate prayer for unity suggests that we are to engage and assemble with other believers to build God-duplicated relationships (John 17). I see Christ's prayer to the Father for his disciples' oneness as the strategy needed for universal reconciliation.

I admit that we have taught (and been taught) in a limited capacity reconciliation in our congregation and region and have not been successful in expanding this ministry to the point that we are practicing multiethnic unity. Yes, the need to go deeper into studying and applying biblical racial reconciliation principles to everyday Christianity is our real hope. Some scriptures that motivate universal reconciliation are as follows: "There is neither Jew nor Greek, there is neither bond nor free, there is neither male nor female for you are all one in Christ Jesus" (Galatians 3:28, NKJV). This scripture implies that God does not divide his followers based on their ethnic identity, economic status, or gender but promotes oneness and togetherness within the Christian camp. Daniel wrote, "And there was given him dominion, and glory, and a kingdom, that all people, nations, and languages, should serve him: his dominion is an everlasting dominion, which shall not pass away, and his kingdom that which shall not be destroyed" (Daniel 7:14, KJV). This scripture prophesied that God's kingdom instituted by Christ will be made up of all individuals representing different nations and languages.

This ministry of racial reconciliation is a call to accountability and moral excellence. As a reconciliation minister, I must be willing to be accountable to the Father for my racial attitudes and unjustified racial behavior. I also must forgive all individuals who oppose me because of who I am or my cultural thinking. I must never compromise God's Word to accommodate unjust agendas, and I cannot afford to remain stuck in erroneous past teachings and hold revenge in my heart due to our painful history. World leaders must learn how to help people with racial barriers. Racial accountability means accepting the fact that someone of one race did something wrong to someone of another race and have taken the responsibility to rectify the situation if the opportunity breeds relevancy. When a person is victimized due to racism and does not receive healing and closure from the oppressor, sinful behavior is bound to resurface or be created. I was richly blessed through these interviews with our ministry leaders. They have positively impacted our practical theology and increased our optimism. I believe that our ministry leaders and congregation want to do what's right, learn more about racial reconciliation, and lead and teach others to demonstrate racial harmony in the world we serve because Jesus's prayer for unity has truly transformed our hearts!

THEME: OTHER INTERVIEW INSIGHTS

Other reconciliation themes emerged from interviews that I had with regional Christian leaders who were not members of our congregation. My aim for this chapter is to summarize their conversations. The need for intentional leadership to implement reconciliation ministry regionally was suggested. Each leader emphasized how crucial, strategic, and impactful intentionality can be if enough leaders are willing to work together to solve the racial disconnect in our area. It is easy to just be with our families and friends, building relationships that we have made over the years with people that look like us, act like us, live in our community, and go to school, work, or church with us. But being intentional about meeting people of different races and cultures allows the Christian to know people that have different upbringings, traditions, foods, and experiences. Personal sacrifices are demanded to accomplish this level of service. The need for effective radical thinking that leads to radical changes in behavior is the love theme that's at the core of racial healing. Many of our congregations exist in segregated communities, and so we lack cultural diversity, which makes it harder to bring diverse people together. A serious observation from these interviews suggests that there are unconscious feelings of ethnic superiority or inferiority that are real when people address racial barriers and problems in their environment.

The conclusion is that there is a need for corrective racial reconciliation theology as it relates to the past teaching of reconciliation theology. All Christians should fully embody Christian reconciliation theology. Being unfair to people of minority races and disadvantaged cultures, being divisive, and ignoring others point to a hole in our Christian theology. The need to accept and follow the direction of the Holy Spirit in building racial harmony within the world was a reiterated theme among all the interviewees. The aggressive cultural breakdown of biblical Christianity by the anti-Christian world has made the theme of Christian unity a top priority today. The call is for the global Christian community to embrace and advance the biblical principles of racial reconciliation theology throughout the world. This book represents the concerns of the Christian leaders that I was blessed to interview and/or dialogue with. It is also my pressing desire and inspiration for establishing a model of restoring, repairing, and rebuilding ethnic relationships within the Christian community and the world we serve. It is a call for an improved, effective, practical, and radical reconciliation theology. It is the core biblical message behind Christ's prayer for unity. It is the articulated voices of non-Christians who desire connectedness with Christians. It is the pain of the next generation articulated. It is the crucial work of the kingdom ambassador explained. It is the heart of the Father revealed. It is my prayer defined, which says there is an urgency to regulate God's plan of action for racial healing and harmony.

RESEARCH FINDINGS

I start this chapter with the conclusion that I am not a reconciliation expert or a bona fide competent researcher, but I see myself and all believers of Christ as reconciliation ministers. Jesus did not call all believers to serve in the capacity of apostles, prophets, evangelists, bishops, pastors, and teachers. He did not give all Christians all the spiritual gifts (1 Corinthians 12:28–31), but he did declare that his disciples will be witnesses for him to the entire world (Acts 1:8). I decided to research this subject of racial reconciliation as a thesis project because I felt that there was an academic gap identifying the application of ethnic harmony in traditional Christian theology. This research has changed my concept of ministry and has evolved into my life's purpose and mission. Racial reconciliation theology has gained my full attention beyond my doctoral work and graduation. There are statements that I have written in this book that is controversial, debatable, and will be rejected. In some themes, I am not theological enough, I sound confused and/or contradictory. However, if you conclude this book with the assertion that racial reconciliation theology needs more research and development, or that the problem of racial disconnect in our world needs to be addressed, or you sense an urgency to fulfill Jesus's prayer for unity among his followers, then my investment in writing this book is not in vain and I have reached my goal for this book.

There are three findings recommended from my research that should motivate further study.

THE NEED FOR PASTORAL LEADERSHIP

The first finding from the interviews suggests that there is a need for pastoral leadership that will prioritize and motivate racial reconciliation as a crucial and urgent ministry of the congregation. It was agreed among the research participants that racial reconciliation is rare in Christian congregations, mainly because it does not qualify as a top priority of the senior pastor and the pastoral staff. Because racial tension is on the rise in America, it is implied that Christian leaders are now challenged to rethink their position to better serve and socialize all parishioners. There is an absence of focus, courage, unity, growth, and intentionality coming from the pulpit that must change if racial healing is to become a reality. The participants I interviewed expressed deep personal concerns because they lack skills in building cross-cultural relationships. They believe that most parishioners want to see effective programming for racial reconciliation coming from the pulpit. It must be noted that it will take mature, wise pastoral leadership to know when the congregation is ready to implement strategies and training for congregational implementation. The advice of leaders of multiethnic congregations suggests that the pastoral staff should have knowledge, experience, and courage that will address the congregational fears related to building race relations.

It was also suggested by most of the participants that the pastoral staff must become leaders in race relations problem-solving, conflict-resolution forums, training for the community and congregation, and staffing qualified pastoral care counselors that are equipped to deal with the pains and anxieties related to racial disunity. Racial reconciliation programs come with monetary costs that must be considered from a pastoral budget perspective. The need for resources and training must become a high-budget priority. Moving the congregation toward a positive influence on program implementation calls for the congregation's stakeholders to approve proper funding for longevity engagement. Transformational leadership is needed to root out and destroy sin in the camp and to humbly build truth, confidence, and the spirit of community among the people. This starts with effective prayer, biblical teaching, and skillful training. I have learned that there are experts in reconciliation ministry and racial healing that can assist the pastoral staff to reach their reconciliation goals.

THE NEED FOR CORRECTIVE EDUCATION, EXPOSURE, AND AWARENESS

The second finding from the interviews suggests that there is a need for bringing corrective education, exposure, and awareness of the political and cultural differences among races as they relate to the Christian community and the world we serve. The painful past of America's race relations continues to hinder progress and the dissolution of racial disunity mainly because of false or wrong information taught within the Christian community and on social media outlets. According to every participant in the study, the history of racism in Christianity has impacted and hindered the progress of racial healing outside of Christianity. There is a stubborn conformity to racism's underlining benefits. Some reasons identified that maintain stubbornness are biblical ignorance, segregation, lack of accountability, lack of focus, lack of love, lack of understanding of other cultures, and the lack of stable Christian upbringing. Other elements of the historical breakdown of races have to do with the reality of stereotyping among all races, the sin of greed, and the absence of effective dialogue among the ethnic groups to analyze and solve their race problems.

Facing this reality is painful because it demands individual growth, personal examination, and assertive learning. Healing the racial divide among us calls for self-denial. It is a cross-bearing agenda that's connected to various forms of suffering and persecution. According to step 2 in the book *Creating Positive Relations*, the agent for racial healing must agree to accept discomfort. Step 2 says, "Assess your willingness to be uncomfortable while you grow to become more competent in dealing with racial issues. Make a conscious decision to accept the discomfort that comes with personal development on this subject."[122] This suggests that all burdens and hesitations about their commitment to fighting racism must be eliminated.

There is already an overwhelming motivation and teaching to change the present narrative by recruiting and training radical Christians to develop a no-nonsense approach to dealing with any future racism. Each Christian must accept this responsibility to be educated and trained as a reconciliation minister. Self-change can be difficult if you are to replace faulty thinking, fears, ungodly behavior, and inherited beliefs. The challenge to love individuals unconditionally and embrace cultural diversity are key components of racial healing. Certain racial epitaphs and jargon should be changed or eliminated. We all come from one race, the human race, with cultural and ethnic distinctiveness. Ethnic differences should be equally embraced and applauded. Therefore, the Christian congregation should promote spiritual oneness and multicultural destinies, which is the epitome of the Body of Christ.

Another observation discussed among the research participants was based on certain historical denominational structures and rules that prohibit multiethnicity, which hinder greater Christian brotherhood. This reality complicates the goal of biblical unity and

---

[122] Taylor Cox Jr. *Creating Positive Race Relations: What You Can Do to Make a Difference* (Bloomington: IN, 2020), 4.

practical Christianity. Each congregation has established norms for worship styles and order of service preferences that varies based on denominational training and practices. The thing to remember is that different cultural and religious groups have different appetites for assembling, and they are not that motivated to change because what works for one particular congregation may not work for another. Embracing different styles of worship can be a positive move toward Christian unity and combating disunity and tension if the worship styles shared are done in spirit and truth.

Geographical locations also play a role in where a person worships. This complicated dilemma is solvable if the congregation is open to adjustments in their styles of worship, which will accommodate everyone who desires to worship with them. I have witnessed the healing of damaged emotions that came from institutionalized racism but was challenged and destroyed through authentic praise and worship because the presence and glory of God inhabit the atmosphere of God's people. My wife and I enjoy visiting different houses of worship to experience not only the praise and worship but also the preaching and giving styles of God's people. We always look for, learn from, and appreciate diversity.

The political climate in America is the core carte blanche for modern-day racial problems according to the participants of this research. We all agreed that American politics drives denominational theology and religious conformity to systemic racism in our world. This is a huge barrier and determinant for the continued hindrance of building a solid racial reconciliation theology. The argument is that internal and external angry trajectories identified within the Christian community violate basic human rights and the biblical command to love one another. Our theology must determine our politics; our politics should not determine our theology. That means that the Christian community must actively advocate for policies that are Bible-based and kingdom driven. And we must "challenge people who show bias in their speech or actions."[123] Paul would say, "The weapons we fight with are not the weapons of the world. On the contrary, they have divine power to demolish strongholds. We demolish arguments and every pretension that sets itself up against the knowledge of God, and we take captive every thought to make it obedient to Christ" (2 Corinthians 10:4–5, NIV). It is the Christian soldier that will endure hardships (2 Timothy 2:3) and prevail in pulling down the political and religious strongholds in our communities and world.

THE NEED FOR A HISTORICAL AND HERMENEUTICAL APPROACH

The third finding derived from the participant interviews and Bible study surveys is that there is a need to apply a correct historical and hermeneutical approach to teaching racial reconciliation to the Christian community. The Bible study used foundational scriptures as the authority for teaching racial reconciliation theology. All participants agree that it is the Christian community that must take responsibility for solving the racial divide among us. We believe that racial disharmony is a sin and is identified in the Bible as such. We believe that all believers should learn to lead the way to the repair of race relations. It is hard to relive a painful past and accept the call to walk in love, forgiveness, and righteousness. The Christian community must embrace this divine passion and teaching on spiritual and racial reconciliation. Ethnic unity is a biblical reconciliation principle. Regardless of how painful and challenging the process may seem, God's expectation of us to be a united force on earth is not a negotiable item. Jesus's conversation with the Samaritan woman in chapter 4 of John's gospel is biblical

---

[123] Cox, *Creating Positive Race Relations*, 52.

evidence and our motivation for the implementation of racial healing and restoration from religious and political division.

Paul's letter to the Galatians informed believers that Christians are to be unified in Christ Jesus as children of God (Galatians 3:28). Daniel's text explains that every ethnic group should serve and worship the God of the universe (Daniel 7:14). James challenged the Christians not to show favoritism to each other or outsiders (James 2:1–13). The book of Ephesians encourages the Christian community to intentionally focus on building true unity of the Spirit (Ephesians 4:3), and the fifth chapter of 2 Corinthians explains how each follower of Christ has an individual obligation to implement a ministry of reconciliation to the unsaved world (2 Corinthians 5:17–21). This approach, which depends mainly on the Christian Bible as the secure mandated manual for achieving and building successful oneness among humanity, has no real competition.

BIBLE STUDY
SURVEY ANALYSIS

After the six-session Bible study, a survey was given to the participants to see if there was an increase in theological knowledge as it relates to dissolving ethnic division that leads to racism. Were there reconciliation strategies and policies to improve established congregational life? A brief summation of the Bible study lessons reveals that the problem statement and thesis purpose was addressed and the need for future advancement in racial reconciliation theology for the Christian community was encouraged. These are my short summations of the focus group's Bible study answers:

What is the scriptural basis for racial reconciliation?

- The sovereignty of God suggests that God supervises the complete relationship-building process (Genesis 11:1–9, Acts 2, Revelations 5:9–10).
- Christ's passion is that Christians should be one as the Father and Jesus are One (John 17:21–23).
- Christians must reach out to all parts of the world to unify the races (Matthew 28:16–20).
- Ephesians 2:8 and 2 Corinthians 5:11–21 are foundational scriptures for Christian unity.
- Philippians 4:3 teaches that Christians can do all things through Christ who gives them strength.

- The Christian's love, faith, and grace are in Christ Jesus, and with these in practice, Christians can overcome racism (1 Corinthians 13).
- Before reconciliation takes place, both parties must have a change of heart toward each other (John 3:16).
- Christians must also recognize that the real fight for racial reconciliation is not against flesh and blood but against unclean spirits in high places (Ephesians 6:12, Corinthians 10:3–5).
- Christians must identify and overcome cultural assumptions in life that have the potential to hinder the spread of the gospel (Romans 15:5–6).
- Righteousness, justice, love, and faithfulness are virtues of God's throne (Psalm 89:14, NIV)
- All believers are saved by grace—it is a gift from God (Ephesians 2:5).
- Christ came to this earth to reconcile humanity back to the Father (Luke 2:7–14, Ephesians 2:14–18, Colossians 1:19–21, Romans 5:10).

What are the biblical blessings connected to racial reconciliation?

- Biblical unity is based on harmony, not uniformity.
- Psalms 133 teaches us the following:
- God is pleased when believers all get along resulting in the gift of eternal life.
- Unity is precious and pleasant in God's eyes.
- Unity produces cooperation, peace, and love.
- Unity is in God.
- Unity teaches that it is praiseworthy when God's children can live together.
- Unity is to experience the sweetness of unconditional love with God and each other.

- Blessings flow when diverse congregations or denominations come together to reconcile as God commanded believers to do.
- Commanded blessings and eternal life are for the community of believers.
- You see the overflow of blessings when believers come together demonstrating humility and empathy.
- Compared to precious oil running down the beard of priests, God's anointing is on unified Christians.
- Divine blessings are for all of God's children who practice oneness.
- Unity is a rare and precious gift through the Holy Spirit.

What are the steps to building positive race relations?

Faith

- Christians must believe in God.
- Christians must receive Jesus Christ as Lord and Savior.
- Christians must believe in Christ Jesus's redemptive work on the cross.
- Christians must believe that all peoples are God's creation.
- All individuals must first believe and receive Christ to enter into the family of God.
- When individuals become believers, they have a new identity "in Christ."
- With faith, we can do cross-culture evangelism.

Fellowship

- Christians cannot love God and not love others.
- Christians must do things together to demonstrate oneness.
- Coming together and seeing no fault or color in each other is Christianity.

- If Christians hate or discriminate, that's an act of walking in darkness.
- True fellowship is the result of being in Christ and Christ being in the believer.
- Christ's blood cleanses everyone of all sin. That will help the believer with building spiritual relationships with people from different backgrounds.
- God is Light. People will see the Light in the believer and be attracted to that Light.
- True fellowship means that quality time is spent with each other.

Friendship

- God wants Christians to love others because Jesus is the greatest friend.
- Christians can become truly intimate friends.
- Friendship is a high level of love.
- Believers are friends of Jesus who obey Christ's commands.
- Christians are called to build positive intimate relationships with Jesus and others.
- One way to love is to lay down one's life for someone else. This includes everyone regardless of race.
- Jesus is the believer's friend and calls us to be friends with each other.

Family

- Whoever does what God wants to be done is in the family of God.
- Those individuals who do the will of God are our spiritual family.
- Jesus's brother, sister, or mother are those who obey the Father.

- All who confess Jesus as Lord is in God's family.
- Your true family is the family of God by creation and some by redemption.
- Family members will occasionally disagree with each other; however, when God's command to love one another is obeyed, disagreements are minimized and resolved.

Forgiveness

- Christians should put aside differences, be kind, and forgive because God has forgiven everyone through Christ Jesus.
- Forgive those who have wronged you and your people.
- Forgiveness can only be attained through Christ's blood.
- If forgiveness does not take place, racial reconciliation will continue to be as it is today, unresolved.
- If the disciple doesn't forgive others, then the father will not forgive the disciple.
- Know that as believers, you have already been forgiven for past, present, and future sins.
- Hatred and bitterness are to be abandoned by the Christian.
- Christians are to be kind and tenderhearted.

What are the divine results of racial reconciliation?

- Christians receive God's grace and power to build godly relationships.
- Favor comes when Christians begin to love and care for one another regardless of skin color or cultural differences.
- God shows favor to his people when the Christian community is committed to fellowshipping together (Acts 2:42–47).
- The divine result of being of one mind and one heart is a manifestation of Christ's mind and heart in the believer.

- Christians receive favor (grace) from God when they imitate God.
- Christians can find favor with God when they imitate him.
- Favor is God's graciousness bestowed upon the faithful.

What are the Christian responsibilities in building better relationships within the Body of Christ?

Personal responsibility

- Some believers must make a change and walk in love.
- Christians must walk worthy of their God-given ministry.
- Christians must be intentional and do what the Word instructs us to do.
- We are commissioned to do all things motivated by the love of God.
- Christians must be teachable.
- Christians should have great patience with others.
- Christians are to live publicly and privately in a manner worthy of the calling on their life.
- Christians must be patient with their growth and development.

Spiritual responsibility

- Be aware and keep the spirit of peace, be a peacemaker.
- Peacemakers are identified as God's children.
- We should strive to maintain unity through peace.
- Christian's feet should be in readiness to spread the gospel of peace.
- The spirit of peace should be with and in the gospel minister.
- Christians are not to grieve the Holy Spirit by holding on to bitterness and evil speaking.

- We are to stay unified in the Spirit.
- Believers must cultivate the spirit of community.
- Christians must hold on to the peace that is beyond all understanding.
- Through prayer, the God of peace will protect your mind and heart.

Doctrinal responsibility

- God gave leaders to the Body of Christ to equip ministers with the fruit of righteousness and Christian unity.
- Christians are to make disciples of every nation. This is the Great Commission.
- Every man and woman of God should live a life according to God's standards.
- Christians are to be lifelong students of scripture.
- The serious student of the Bible will continue to grow in God's Word and become a mature follower of Christ.
- Christ gave the believer divine power, talent, and abilities to be equipped for works of service so that believers may attain the whole measure of the fullness of Christ.
- We have one Lord and one faith to keep us grounded in the Word of God.
- It is shameful for a Christian to wrongly divide God's Word.

Moral responsibility

- Believers are to seek moral excellence.
- Believers must change for the better by renewing their minds daily to do what is right.
- Believers are to do good work for the kingdom of God.
- Believers must ask the Holy Spirit to control their mouths so they can speak the truth in love.
- Believers are not to transgress against God's covenant.

- Believers are not allowed to harbor anger that leads to sin.
- Being reconciled to God makes it possible to live a God-honoring lifestyle that reconciles others to God. This can be called lifestyle evangelism.
- Believers must continue to walk in the light and not in darkness, be in the world but not of the world.
- Believers are to do nothing that keeps other believers from building each other up.
- Believers are created to be like God in true righteousness and holiness.
- Once a believer has experienced the life of a reconciliation minister, no other life is worth living.

CORRECTIVE RACIAL RECONCILIATION THEOLOGY

The advancement of basic relevant scriptural knowledge of the theology of racial reconciliation was the goal of the research and this goal, on a comprehensible level, was met. The racial reconciliation ministry has a direct connection to spiritual reconciliation theology. The validation and awareness of the interwovenness of ethnic identities into biblical narratives connected to the redemptive work of Jesus Christ helped me to understand this assumption. This research claims that there is a progressive revelation in scripture that suggests a need for the repairing of ethnic (race) relations among God's people and in the world. The command to reach the world with the gospel of Christ is the very heartbeat of racial reconciliation theology.

God is a relational God who promotes positive relationships among his creation. These notes from the interviews represent God's timeless expectations for building relationships with divinity and humanity. I have summarized selected information from the participant's interviews that validate our assumptions of God's expectations:

1. We are all created to represent God's imagery.
2. Racial reconciliation should be a ministry for all believers of Jesus Christ.

3. God's Word teaches the children of God to be one in nature.
4. Jesus's prayer and passion are for his followers to be a spiritually unified force on earth like him and the Heavenly Father.
5. Redemption is an action word revealed in the believer's character and conduct.
6. Love is the Christian's identification in a hateful world.
7. The believer's priority is to live a life of faith in God and his Word.

God, being the chief reconciler, reconciled the world back to the desired relationship through Jesus Christ and has given the believer the corresponding ministry of reconciliation (2 Corinthians 5:18). The believer is God's earthly representative, Christ's ambassador with the assignment of connecting divine favor to this sinful world (2 Corinthians 5:18–6:1). The believer is to evangelize the entire world and make disciples for Christ from all nations (Matthew 28:19). A strategic model for evangelizing all races is given by Jesus, who said to his disciples, "You shall receive power when the Holy Spirit has come upon you, and you shall be witnesses to Me in Jerusalem, and in all Judea and Samaria, and the end of the earth" (Acts 1:8, NKJV). I'm convinced that the disciple of Jesus Christ should pursue the task of building better communities by building God-approved relationships that represent the kingdom of God.

It is the Bible-based believer that this book is challenging to go out into the neighborhoods and be the gospel (the good news) that demonstrates to people of all colors and cultures the true love and passion of the universal God. This is important because when people of other marginalized races are ignored by Christ's community, the barriers of divisiveness, unfairness, and oppression remain embedded in our experiences as acceptable Christian theology. I am convinced that the key to accomplishing racial reconciliation is to remove the hindrances and roadblocks that isolate individuals from the true spirit of civility.

Jesus demonstrated multiethnic healing and cross-cultural evangelism in the fourth chapter of John. According to the narrative, Jesus had a conversation with a Samaritan woman. The significance of this conversation has layers of meaning, as mentioned earlier. The ethnic-related observation that Jesus challenged was the notion that "Jews do not associate with Samaritans" (John 4:9, NIV). The Samaritans were looked at by the Jews as demon-possessed people (John 8:48). An aspect of Jesus's redemptive plan included loving all individuals, even those that the religious communities had rejected. Luke wrote that Jesus was anointed with the Holy Spirit and power "who went about doing good and healing all who were oppressed by the devil, for God was with Him" (Acts 10:38, NKJV). Jesus's conversation with the Samaritan woman resulted in a new way of communicating with this multiracial community. We can learn from this text how Jesus's intentionality and boldness to build a relationship with this woman broke the traditional cultural and religious norms of his day (John 4:39–43).

Furthermore, the implication and application of this text suggest that the Christian community can pursue a hope that is designed to destroy present-day anti-multiculturalism and racial disconnect. In this text, Jesus demonstrated to the disciples that there is a level of redemptive work that is the will of God but must be progressively manifested (John 4:3–135). I suggest that what Jesus demonstrated is corrective racial (ethnic) reconciliation.

It must be a conviction, a personal act of courageous faith that the follower of Christ uses to advance and pave the path to building kingdom relationships. He/she must move with the understanding that the kingdom of God is divinely made up of all ethnic groups within the human race. Racial reconciliation theology accommodates the leader who represents a holy and righteous Father who instructs all of his creation to live in peaceful harmony now and throughout eternity (Psalm 133). Unity among the human race has always been rare and a struggle since the fall of humanity (Genesis 3). It intensified through God's judgment against the building of the tower of Babel (Genesis 11:1–9). God confused their language and scattered them throughout the earth, thus making the reconciliation of ethnicity, which is an aspect of the ministry of reconciliation, a task only God can supervise. Most individuals tend to stay away from racial reconciliation directives because of the incompetence of humanity to solve the problem of deep-rooted mistrust among races (ethnic groups). There is a high personal cost connected to biblical cross-cultural communication. The need for accurate revelation, spiritual discernment, and the demand for humility are qualities that are necessary for true racial reconciliation advocacy. The Bible is not silent! It attacks ungodly divisions and motives behind all evil behavior. It informs the believer that fights and wars originate because of individuals who crave worldly friendships and selfish pleasures.[124] James wrote, "You adulterous people, don't you know that friendship with the world is hatred towards God? Anyone who chooses to be a friend of the world becomes an enemy of God" (James 4:4, NIV). The enemy of Christian unity will always seek to create divisions among the followers of Christ. Beneath the surface of racism is an agenda of selfishness that erects institutionalized boundaries that safeguard one group's wealth while limiting another group's livelihood. These individuals who exhibit such behavior are stuck in unethical and unbiblical retrodiction. The challenge is for the entire Christian community to seek to work together to destroy those barriers or boundaries that keep individuals from engaging, supporting, and loving each other.

The risk of promoting racial reconciliation theology is real. The reconciliation minister must be aware of the fact that bringing up past racial problems normally will open up old wounds that can result in backlash from people that is against or don't understand racial reconciliation theology enough to support it. The minister's focus is Jesus's prayer in John 17 which reveals the Christological

---

[124] Read James 4:1–12.

passion to make the community of believers a powerful unified influence on this earth.

Our Heavenly Father and the incarnate Son's relationship defines and demonstrates true oneness recommended for us, the Christian community, to duplicate (John 17:22–23). Who is willing to pursue this ministry to advance the kingdom of God on this earth? Can you embrace Christ's prayer and make it your vision? Can you see a society where God's children have learned to live together in harmony with all their neighbors? This represents a lifestyle based on God's anointed secured blessings. The challenge for the reconciliation minister is to separate from all platforms of unbelief, unrighteousness, and false fellowships that disrupt the connectedness of God's entire family. As we transparently recognize our relationship with the Father, he will receive us as his spiritual sons and daughters (2 Corinthians 6:14–18). This biblical truth makes reconciliation theology worth studying because every one of us (all humans) has sinned and at one time lived a life alienated from God, thus qualifying us for his gift of redemptive love and restorative empathy that only God, through Christ Jesus, can give us and that we the recipients of his grace can give the world.

STEPS TO RACIAL RECONCILIATION

To deal with past mistakes as it relates to the racial dysfunction in the Christian community and the world is to seek to understand how segregation evolved and played a role in limiting ethnic diversity and harmony in the world, and then rectify it. Believers must accept the responsibility for the part that the Christian community played in supporting the system that for hundreds of years destroyed families of color. This journey comes with a gigantic price tag that many Christians are not willing to pay. This research concludes that many Christians are not willing to be uncomfortable with racial problems and that others feel that the price is just too high. Humans normally gravitate toward what is comfortable and not always what is biblically expected and/or mandated. The crucial point to grasp is the notion that many spiritual leaders don't know where to start or what to do to be successful in racial reconciliation programs and initiatives. Therefore, a biblical, workable solution is needed and desired based on the findings of this research. These are suggestive steps to be considered as a roadmap to building better relationships within the Christian community and the world we serve.

STEP 1: DEMONSTRATING FAITH IN CHRIST

Stemming from this research are suggestive practical steps to building godly Christian relationships. The process must start with demonstrating faith in the written word of God that presents the gospel of Jesus Christ. John wrote, "He came to His own, and His own did not receive Him. But as many as received Him, to them He gave the right to become children of God, to those who believe in His name: who were born, not of blood, nor of the will of man, but of God" (John 1:11–13, NKJV). Jesus's ethnic group initially rejected him as the Messiah, but this paved the way for other ethnic groups who believed and received his kingdom message to become part of God's family of believers. Those who believe are born through the Spirit of God into the family of God. This principle has not changed; everyone who believes in Christ experiences spiritual birth and eternal life (John 3:1–21). To win a soul to the family of God, we should follow Jesus's example of bold intentionality. To be intentional is to be accountable (Romans 1:14–16). It is the prompting of the Holy Spirit that will bring bold intentionality to the believer to win souls into the family of God. The benefits resulting from the believer's faith to reach out to other races are enormous. Meeting and dialoguing with people of different races and cultures allows the reconciliation minister to know and experience people that have different upbringings, traditions, foods, and experiences. This experience is priceless because it enhances the skill of relationship building and it substantiates the Great Commission.

Every disciple of Christ must also learn to be a discipler for Christ and recognize that "there is no difference between Jew and Gentile-the same Lord is Lord of all and richly blesses all who call on him, for, everyone who calls on the name of the Lord will be saved" (Romans 10:12–13, NIV). The real job of the believer (the reconciliation minister) is to preach, teach, and mimic Christ. Following Christ means taking on the mind, attitude, actions, and characteristics of the Son of God and applying his teaching to everyday activities. Jesus's earthly ministry gave the world a perfect example by showing us how to demonstrate love for all people and to treat all of them as God's precious people. Each believer has an amazing opportunity to show the realness of Christ's redemptive love through the endorsed interknitting of God's people. With this thought in mind, racial reconciliation ministry starts with the believer's commitment to evangelism (being a witness for Christ) that spreads outward to draw all kinds of people into God's love (Acts 1:8). It is the empowerment of the Holy Spirit and faith in Christ for salvation that crystallizes the beginning of a genuine relationship with the Father and with all of his human creation.

STEP 2: VALIDATING RELATIONSHIPS THROUGH FELLOWSHIP

The second step in the relationship-building approach is to not only pursue God and enjoy his companionship but also to seek other believers' company through activities that produce meaningful fellowship. Christians who love and obey Christ will be blessed with constant fellowship with the Father and Son. Jesus informed his disciples, "If anyone loves me, he will obey my teaching. My Father will love him, and we will come to him and make our home with him" (Jn. 14:23, NIV). What a great promise; however, this Christian fellowship (*koinonia*) is not only with the Father and the Son but also with other believers through the Spirit of God. John wrote, "If we walk in the light, as he is in the light, we have fellowship with one another, and the blood of Jesus, his Son, purifies us from all sin" (1 John 1:7, NIV).

On the subject of Christian fellowship, we have a divine assignment to go into all nations and talk to all people and get to know their likes and dislikes and make them disciples of Christ.

God desires to bring disconnected people together for heavenly-affirmed fellowship. This fellowship is very important to God. He wants us to experience the power of agreement, the legitimacy of togetherness, and the stability of the Body of Christ. This call to community building communicates the foundational ingredient needed for reconciliation advancement. No one can successfully separate reconciliation principles from the believer's relationship with the Father, the Son, and the diverse family of believers. Believers are technically united because the Bible teaches that we are one in Spirit, and this unity of spirit represents the replica of trinitarian fellowship. From a practical perspective, we must reckon ourselves dead to disunity and alive as a consolidated organism. The racial reconciliation minister craves positive relationship-building, explorative social change, and approved interventions that breed healthy spiritual partnerships. This unity is possible because it is the Spirit of God that gives life to the minister. Paul wrote, "He has made us competent as ministers of a new covenant-not of the letter but of the Spirit; for the letter kills, but the Spirit gives life" (2 Corinthians 3:6, NIV). It is the Spirit of God that makes us competent ministers of the new covenant.

The challenge for the reconciliation minister is to spend quality time daily with God and with other believers. The infant church in Acts 2 fellowshipped daily together in the temple and from house to house (Acts 2:46). God daily added to the Christian community as their relationships matured by spending quality time with each other (v. 47). In the development of the Christian community, submergence of awareness of economic and social issues challenged the entire community of believers. Spending time with all the converts helped the more stable Christians to identify the personal needs of the group and to meet them. True fellowship is the combination of the believer being in Christ and the life of Christ dwelling in the hearts of the believers to render corporate mutual support and activity to those with unmet needs with no strings attached.

STEP 3: DEEPENING FRIENDSHIPS

The third step to building godly relationships is when secrecy, intimacy, and loyalty in the relationship mature to the level of friendship. Jesus said, "Greater love has no one than this than to lay down one's life for his friends … No longer do I call you servants, for a servant does not know what his master is doing; but I have called you friends, for all things that I heard from my Father I have made known to you" (John 15:13, 15:15, NKJV). Jesus changed the dynamics of the master-and-servant (*kurios* and *doulos*) relationship with friends (*philos*). This is a major shift in the relationship-building process. Complete honesty and transparency complement the union. This calls for a high level of Christian compassion and legitimate concern for the well-being of each other.

Personal sacrifices for each other in the relationship become the spoken as well as the unspoken norms. David and Jonathan exemplified the uniqueness and loyalty that are precious qualities that characterize godly relationships (1 Samuel 20). The text says that Jonathan loved David: "He loved him as he loved himself" (v. 17, NIV). In David's Song of the Bow, David's declaration of the relationship explains the power behind godly covenant relationships. David said, "I am distressed for you, my brother Johnathan; you have been very pleasant to me; your love to me was wonderful, surpassing the love of women" (2 Samuel 1:26, NKJV). This realization of a personal obligation to care for and share passionate truths solidifies spiritual cronyism that can only be accomplished through authentic Christian friendships.

Paul informed his readers, "Don't team up with those who are unbelievers. How can righteousness be a partner with wickedness? How can light live with darkness? What harmony can there be between Christ and the Devil? How can a believer be a partner with an unbeliever? And what union can there be between God's temple and idols?" (2 Corinthians 6:14–16, NLT). The challenge is for the believer to understand that there is a big difference between his/her interactions with God's family and his/her interactions with the unbelieving community. Christian friendships are based on God's eternal covenant that cannot be paralleled with affiliation with the unsaved world. Paul went on to explain that we are the habitation of the living God and that God said, "I will live in them and walk among them, I will be their God, and they will be my people. Therefore, come out from among unbelievers, and separate yourselves from them, says the Lord. Don't touch their filthy things, and I will welcome you. And I will be your Father, and you will be my sons and daughters, says the Lord Almighty" (2 Corinthians 6:16–18, NLT). The application of this text is to put Christian maturity on display by prioritizing kingdom relationships as of greater value than all other relationships.

STEP 4: ENGAGING THE FAMILY

The fourth step to building godly relationships is the acceptance of all believers not only for fellowship and as friends but also as family members in God's family. Jesus asked, "Who is My mother, and who are My brothers?" His response was, "Whoever does the will of My Father in heaven is My brother and sister, and mother" (Matthew 12:48, 12:50, NKJV). A member of God's family portrays family values (John 19:26–27). Jesus instructed John to assume the role of a son in Mary's life when Jesus could no longer do it. In the Christian family, there are times when members of the family need strength, resources, and encouragement. Jesus demonstrated this with Peter. Not only did Peter need to be prayed for, but he was also instructed to affectionately do the same for other members of Christ's spiritual family. Jesus said to Peter, "Satan has asked for you, that he may sift you as wheat. But I have prayed for you, that your faith should not fail; and when you have returned to Me, strengthen your brethren" (Luke 22:31–32, NKJV). *Brethren* (*adelphos* in Greek) means a fellow believer, united to another by the bond of affection.

The noticeable sign of a mature member of God's family is the ability to recognize and accept that God has spiritual sons and daughters from all nations of the world. More insight into the family of God is found in the book of Romans. Paul wrote, "For all who are led by the Ruach Elohim, these are sons of God. For you did not receive the spirit of slavery to fall again into fear; rather, you received the Spirit of adoption, by whom we cry, 'Abba! Father!' The Ruach Himself bears witness with our spirit that we are children of God. And if children, also heirs-heirs of God and joint-heirs with Messiah-if indeed we suffer with Him so that we may also be glorified with Him" (Romans 8:14–17, TLV). What comes with this step in the relationship-building process is a true identification with God's spiritual family that comes with the sharing of Christ's inheritance, his suffering, and his glory.

STEP 5: DEMONSTRATE FORGIVENESS

The fifth step to building godly relationships within the Christian community is dissolving past failures and mistakes by Christians that hindered past biblical racial reconciliation advancements. I decided to place this step at the end of the therapeutic process because forgiveness and maturity are synonymous when it comes to repairing and/or restoring broken relationships. The Christian community cannot have unity if the problems that divide the believers are not addressed effectively. This study has revealed that some of the modern barriers to racial reconciliation within the Christian community are selfish politics, a lack of biblical knowledge, and fake forgiveness. We cannot afford to neglect these issues any longer. Paul wrote, "As the elect of God, holy and beloved, put on tender mercies, kindness, humility, meekness, longsuffering; bearing with one another, and forgiving one another, if anyone has a complaint against another; even as Christ forgave you, so you also must do" (Colossians 3:12–13, NKJV). When Christians allow God's love to be manifested in their hearts and their actions, ungodly behavior patterns and petty differences among races are resolved.

To the Ephesians, Paul wrote, "Be kind to each other, tenderhearted, forgiving one another, just as God through Christ has forgiven you" (Ephesians 4:32, NLT). We the research team conclude that the Christian who is unable to forgive is immature and in demonical bondage. We believe that the important scenario for kingdom advancement is to encourage an atmosphere that focuses on reconciling damaged race relations by acknowledging past attacks and sins made against victims of racism. Racial healing occurs when the offending race and the offended race accept the apology (the two sides to forgiveness) as genuine and create a covenant based on love to never return to the offense again. This work is done by the Holy Spirit in the hearts of both believers (Romans 5:5). The Christian community also must accept responsibility for its role in supporting systemic racism. The racial problems in America will not change until more individuals embrace racial healing through responsible institutionalized forgiveness. The model prayer of Jesus teaches all followers of Christ to ask the Father for forgiveness as our forgiveness for others is implemented (Matthew 6:12). The challenging reality is that if the follower of Christ doesn't forgive others, then the Heavenly Father will withhold his forgiveness (v. 14–15). Therefore, forgiveness on both sides of the fence is the critical step to helping the Christian community bring closure to racial disunity and unsolved racial problems.

Applied forgiveness is the evidence of spiritual maturity and the manifestation of spiritual unity. Forgiveness (*aphesis*) is the act of removing the penalty from the guilty individual. This is rarely done by novice Christians. Immature individuals speak forgiveness but refuse to submit to a change in thinking and behavior. Living a life of forgiveness means you give (if you are the oppressor) or receive (if you are the victim of oppression) unlimited freedom from revenge and retaliation. Always remember that we receive unlimited grace and mercy daily from the Father (Psalms 68:19, 23:6). There are many hindrances to race-related forgiveness. One major barrier to Christian unity is an immature, unforgiving heart that spreads discord and dissension among believers (Proverbs 6:19). Paul had to rebuke the Corinthian believers for disunity and immaturity within their congregation. The indictment was that there were contentions within the congregation: Some followed Paul, some followed Apollos, some followed Cephas, and some followed Christ only (1 Corinthians 1:11–12). Since Christ is not divided, then the Christian congregation should not function as carnal people (babes in Christ), guilty of envy, strife, and divisions (1 Corinthians 3:1–3). Each believer must do their part by taking on certain responsibilities that promote and enhance corporate forgiveness and spiritual maturity within the Body of Christ, resulting in divine favor on God's people.

CONCLUSION

The Christian community must share the gospel of Jesus Christ with all people by empowering each believer to focus on a personal evangelistic campaign that embraces a true racial reconciliation ministry. Too, too many believers are closed to the very idea of Christian multiculturalism. It must be understood that personal and corporate growth is needed in most Christians' lives before implementing a program of racial reconciliation. This book suggests that there is a theological position that justifies the Christian who takes a position to help build positive race relationships in this world. This ministry of lovingly reaching out to all ethnic groups is a serious game changer for Christendom.

The informed Christian must be transparent about individual learned behavior patterns of biases and prejudices that have hindered past progress. One suggestion is to take time to listen and follow anointed voices that prioritize racial reconciliation learning. There must be a personal conviction from established leadership that motivates congregants to get involved and take ownership of updated racial problems. Throughout this book, I have reiterated that the Bible is an instructional manual for the racial reconciliation believer (minister). There is an overwhelming amount of scriptures that directly or indirectly claim racial reconciliation ministry as a mandated ministry for the believer of Jesus Christ. Examination of the scriptures gave me enough information to assert the truth that helped facilitate the evolved reconciliation principles derived from this study. I see this book as an aid for the reconciliation minister who sees the need to improve their congregational life, individual growth, and ministry development.

The practical side to developing an effective racial reconciliation ministry starts with the understanding that the reconciliation minister must accept a personal responsibility to live a life that is worthy of the Christian calling (Ephesians 4:1). Christlike character, spiritual birthing, formation, and maturity must be at the core of the minister's lifestyle (Galatians 4:19). The reconciliation minister must imitate God and walk in love on this earth (Ephesians 5:1–2, Galatians 5:14) and make every effort to maintain spiritual unity in the bond of peace (Ephesians 4:3). This godly peace is the righteous spiritual fruit that must be manifested in the Christian character (Galatians 5:22, Matthew 5:9). The warning is clear to the Christian community: "If you bite and devour one another, beware lest you be consumed by one another" (Galatians 5:15, NKJV). The gifted Christian leadership has the responsibility to grow all believers into mature saints, making them one community of believers. Christ gave gifted men to the Christian community to develop the saints to do the work of ministry as a team with perfect unity (Ephesians 4:11–16).

Doctrinal unity is the recipe for congregational stability so that "we will no longer be infants, tossed back and forth by the waves, and blown here and there by every wind of teaching, and by the cunning and craftiness of men in their deceitful scheming" (Ephesians 4:14, NIV). The truth that cannot be compromised is that "there is one body and one Spirit-just as you were called to one hope when you were called-one Lord, one faith, one baptism; one God and Father of all, who is over all, and through all and in all" (Ephesians 4:4–6, NIV). I see in this text the significance of the interwovenness of God's Word as it is connected to the praiseworthiness given to the Spirit, Son, and Father for their unique contributions to bringing unity to the Body of Christ.

The Christian has a moral responsibility to represent a moral God. James wrote, "Get rid of all moral filth and the evil that is so prevalent and humbly accept the word planted in you, which can save you" (James 1:21, NIV). Once saved, the Christian "should no longer walk as the rest of the Gentiles walk in the futility of their minds" (Ephesians 4:17, NKJV). This means that the unsaved self, which is corrupted with deceitful desires, is abandoned and the new self that is created in true righteousness and holiness by God is embraced and empowered to direct the Christian life (Ephesians 4:22–24, NKJV). This new self must be renewed in the spirit of the mind (Ephesians 4:23, Romans 12:2) and continuously impart the practical moral directives suggested by Paul (Ephesians 4:.25–32). There is a legitimate need and demand for more reconciliation ministers and theologians to surface and make a commitment to the expansion of the reconciliation ministry. The charge is to intentionally go into all the world and preach the Good News of the kingdom of God to all races (ethnic groups); and take responsibility for any disunity in the Body of Christ by imitating God and promoting a life of love, understanding, and forgiveness among all peoples.

I started this research with the focus of bringing effective teaching, awareness, and application of the racial reconciliation ministry to the community of believers. The need for biblical doctrine and effective methodology on racial reconciliation was my major concern. I also sought to impress upon God's global family that to be a follower of Christ, they too should exemplify a passion to champion racial reconciliation as a requirement of the Christian life. This book addressed the need for more historical, psychological, and theological research on racial reconciliation. Racial reconciliation ministers must do the work of evangelism and apply a dignity-based, integrity-driven, workable solution to the racial disconnect in the Christian community and the world we serve. I'm convinced that there is a moral responsibility at work within every informed believer to promote and educate all Christians on the topic of racial unity as a unique quality of the Christian life. This research has developed and acknowledged practicalities that can lead us away from the ignorance and arrogance found in racial disparities into the engagement of a racial reconciliation theology that produces support and rationale for advancing this Christ-centered agenda.

In the process of writing this book, I had to contend with the reality that there was a limited amount of material that championed the understanding of biblical racial reconciliation principles. I thank God for the voices, issues, needs, and concerns of the participants in this study that convinced me that an attempt to understand and address the magnitude of the problem was part of my God-ordained assignment. I don't see myself as an expert in this area but as an evolving researcher who is committed to learning and sharing more information on this subject. This research validated the assumption that the racial problems within the Christian community and society are not going anywhere until enough individuals take the position to declare that enough is enough. We share our passion and determination with corporate optimism to join us as we make the shift from a problem-based mindset to a solution-based agenda.

APPLICATION OF THE FINDINGS

Numerous biblical narratives validate God's desire for a unified Christian community in the world he created. For example, in Paul's attempt to dissolve disunity in the Philippian church, an appeal for healing the church's torn relationships prevailed. Paul wrote, "If you have any encouragement from being united with Christ, if any comfort from his love, if any fellowship with the Spirit, if any tenderness and compassion, then make my joy complete by being like-minded, having the same love, being one in spirit and purpose. Do nothing out of selfish ambition or vain conceit, but in humility consider others better than yourselves. Each of you should look not only to your own interests, but also to the interests of others" (Philippians 2:1–4, NIV). The Message Bible says, "If you've gotten anything at all out of following Christ, if his love has made any difference in your life, if being in a community of the Spirit means anything to you, if you have a heart, if you care-then do me a favor: Agree with each other, love each other, be deep-spirited friends. Don't push your way to the front; don't sweet-talk your way to the top. Put yourself aside, and help others get ahead. Don't be obsessed with getting your own advantage. Forget yourselves long enough to lend a helping hand" (Philippians 2:1–4, MSG). This text reveals four principles that can produce unity among the people of God: (1) Christlike humility, (2) Christlike love, (3) fellowship with the Spirit of God, and (4) Christlike fellowship.

CHRISTLIKE HUMILITY

The first principle to be applied is the exhortation (encouragement) for unity that's called Christlike humility. Paul said to the Philippians, "Your attitude should be the same as that of Christ Jesus: Who being in the very nature God, did not consider equality with God something to be grasped, but made himself nothing, taking the very nature of a servant, being made in human likeness. And being found in appearance as a man, he humbled himself and became obedient to death even death on a cross" (Philippians 2:5–8, NIV). Paul's encouragement (*paraklesis*) to the Philippians was to not only obey Christ's teaching but to also follow an example of righteous humility (*tapinofrosoonay*), that lowliness of mind that emptied (*kenosis*) Christ of divine majesty.[125] This demonstration of Christ's selflessness is of the highest excellent form of New Testament Christologies.[126] Paul suggested that the Philippian congregation follow this pattern of humble submission toward each other. Reconciliation ministry facilitators must help Christians to empty themselves of their egos and preconceived perceptions before they can confront disunity in the Body of Christ.

---

[125] Jerry Vines, *The Vines Expository Bible* (Nashville: Thomas Nelson, 2018), 1725.
[126] Ibid.

Matthew reported Jesus's humble exhortation. Jesus said, "Take my yoke upon you and learn from me, for I am gentle and humble in heart, and you will find rest for your souls. For my yoke is easy and my burden is light" (Matthew 11:29–30, NIV). Note that Jesus is gentle and humble in heart. Inward humility is needed to produce outward submission. On another occasion, Jesus challenged the disciples to lead a life of Christlike humility and servanthood. After washing their feet, he put on his robe again, sat down, and asked, "Do you understand what I was doing? You call me Teacher and Lord, and you are right, because that's what I am. And since I, your Lord and Teacher, have washed your feet, you ought to wash each other's feet. I have given you an example to follow. Do as I have done to you. I tell you the truth, slaves are not greater than their master. Nor is the messenger more important than the one who sends the message. Now that you know these things, God will bless you for doing them" (John 13:12–17, NLT). I insert that the Christian leader who can humble himself with Christlike humility and serve others is applauded by men and is highly favored by God.

Paul explained this Christological humility (*trapeinos*) and submission (*hupotasso*) as they relate to family and congregational leadership in the letter to the Ephesians: "Husbands love your wives, just as Christ loved the church and gave himself up for her to make her holy, cleansing her by the washing with water through the word, and to present her to himself as a radiant church, without stain or wrinkle or any other blemish, but holy and blameless" (Ephesians 5:25–27, NIV). Christlike humility is a byproduct of Christlike thinking that instructs the believer to embrace, submit, accept and love each other. Christlike humility starts the flow of reflective grace, mutual love, and honest respect for all of God's creation. Christian diversity should not detour Christians from being like-minded (*autosphroneo*). According to Strong's Concordance,[127] to be "like-minded" means to be of the same mind, to agree, to cherish the same views,

---

[127] James Strong, *Strong's Exhaustive Concordance of the Bible* (Nashville: Thomas Nelson, 1990), 44.

to be harmonious, and to seek one's interest or advantage. Christian disunity and divisions are dismantled when like-minded Christians learn to dwell together with empathy and humility.

CHRISTLIKE LOVE

The second principle to be applied is comfort from Christ's love in the heart of the believer that's manifested toward other believers and the world. According to the book of Romans, "God has poured out his love into our hearts by the Holy Spirit, whom he has given us" (Romans 5:5, NIV). With agape as one of the believer's core ingredients to process spirituality, the believer is engaged with present moment aliveness to God's loving initiatives and step-by-step processes within the Christian community and the world.[128] Boa believes that a genuine response to what God is doing in the Christian life is of critical importance,[129] and that life in Christ is the manifested life of Christ in the believer loving the world, which is kingdom living being active in the present and future realities.[130] Therefore, the love and life of Christ must be realized, renewed, and restored in modern-day Christianity.

A hindrance to Christian unity is the absence of agape among political preachers, many professed believers, and also in some Christian academic circles. Regardless of the spiritual gifts and abilities that accompany the Christian character if love is missing the motive for Christian service is flawed, it is useless, and the Christian is unprofitable in God's eyes. Love is that spiritual fruit that unifies God's people (Galatians 5:22), and should be manifested in every believer (1 Thessalonians 4:9, 1 John 4:7–8). The Christian ambassador is divinely equipped and assigned to love and serve the

---

[128] Kenneth Boa, *Conformed to His Image: Biblical and Practical Approaches to Spiritual Formation* (Grand Rapids: Zondervan, 2001), 255.

[129] Ibid, 257.

[130] Ibid, 265.

world with the message of reconciliation (2 Corinthians 5:19). Paul informs the Christian community, "Christ's love controls us. Since we believe that Christ died for all, we also believe that we have all died to our old life. He died for everyone so that those who receive his new life will no longer live for themselves. Instead, they will live for Christ, who died and was raised for them" (2 Corinthians 5:14–15, NLT). Because of this constraining force in the believer's heart, the believer takes on the qualities of unconditional love and servanthood to build God's kingdom and God's people on this earth. Romans 8:37–39 challenges the reconciliation minister to let nothing separate him/her from the divine love of God.

In Paul's description of agape, he wrote, "Love is patient, love is kind. It does not envy, it does not boast, it is not proud. It is not rude, it is not self-seeking, it is not easily angered, it keeps no record of wrongs. Love does not delight in evil but rejoices with the truth. It always protects, always trusts, always hopes, always perseveres. Love never fails" (1 Corinthians 13:4–8, NIV). This Christlike love is greater than faith (dependence on God) and hope (focusing on a brighter day) because agape is the very nature of God (1 Corinthians 13:13; 1 John 4:8). Christlike love also calls for a maturing of the believer. Paul explained in this love chapter, "When I was a child, I talked like a child, I thought like a child, I reasoned like a child. When I became a man, I put childish ways behind me" (1 Corinthians 13:11, NIV). I believe that it will take loving, mature Christians (not infants in Christ, 1 Corinthians 3:1–4) to embrace and apply racial reconciliation principles and corrective theology for racial healing within the Christian community and the world.

FELLOWSHIP WITH THE SPIRIT OF GOD

The third principle to be applied is fellowship with the Spirit of God, which directs the believers to come together to choose right and do right. The Holy Spirit that comes from the Father to bear witness of

Christ to the world is in the believer as the Spirit of Truth (John14:17, 15:26). The work of the Holy Spirit is to reprove the world of sin, righteousness, and judgment (John 16:8, KJV). The Amplified text reads, "And when He comes, He will convict and convince the world and bring demonstration to it about sin and about righteousness-uprightness of heart and right standing with God-and about judgment" (John 16:8, AMP). The practical side of Christian unity is based on the believer's ability to be an advocate and supporter of the Holy Spirit's work to advance Christ's prayer for unity (John 17:22). This means that the believer must grow spiritually into a mature follower of the Holy Spirit. Paul explained, "For all who are led by the Spirit of God are children of God" (Romans 14:8, NLT). It is the Spirit of God that pours agape into the hearts of the believers (Romans 5:5). It is the Spirit of God that teaches the follower of Christ all things and brings Christ's words back into memory. "He will teach you all things. And he will cause you to recall-will remind you of, bring to your remembrance-everything I have told you" (John 14:25, AMP). Spiritual oneness is not only a passionate prayer of Christ (John 17:20–21) and an exhortation of the apostle Paul (Ephesians 4:13), but it is also the acclimatization of the collaboration of the Holy Spirit's work in the church and the world (Revelations 22:17).

CHRISTLIKE FELLOWSHIP

The fourth principle to be applied engages the believers to unite with one another through qualities of tenderness and compassion received from Christ for others. When these qualities prevail among Christians, divisions disappear, and unity prevails.[131] Paul wanted to encourage the Philippian Christians to live in harmony and oneness. The Amplified text says, "So by whatever [appeal

---

[131] Kenneth Wuest, *Wuest's Word Studies: From the Greek New Testament vol. 3* (Grand Rapids: Wm. B. Eerdmans Publishing Company, 1973), 112.

to you there is in our mutual dwelling in Christ, by whatever] strengthening and consoling and encouraging [our relationship] in Him [affords]. By whatever persuasive incentive there is in love, by whatever participation in the (Holy) Spirit [we share] and by whatever depth of affection and compassionate sympathy, fill up and complete my joy by living in harmony and being of the same mind and one in purpose, having the same love, being in full accord and of one harmonious mind and intention" (Philippians 2:1–2, AMP). No organization can compare to or compete with a considerate, caring, Spirit-led, and Christ-centered congregation that promotes racial unity as a loving haven, a light in this dark, hateful, and hostile world for all peoples.

The NIV text uses the words *tenderness* and *compassion* to explain the attributes of Christlike fellowship. Homer A. Kent Jr. suggested that the understanding of the text should read, "If any fellowship (let it be) of spirit; if any (such fellowship), (let it be) tender mercies and compassions!"[132] Therefore, manifested Christlike humility, Christlike love, partnership with the Spirit of God, and Christlike fellowship are qualities that affirm the Christian character and the Christian community. These are the seeds that are already planted, paving the path upward toward racial reconciliation and multiethnic healing in the Christian community and the world we serve. The call for the reconciliation minister to keep forming meaningful relationships with all races (ethnic groups) through spiritual empowerment, mutual engagement, and biblical wisdom is applauded in this book.

In summary, ethnic harmony and effective Christian relationship-building have been missing and craved ingredients to spiritual reconciliation in American Christianity but are now being addressed with a practical approach through corrective racial reconciliation theology. I pass this baton to the next spiritual warrior who understands that this victory will not be awarded to the swift or the mighty but to the ones who endure to the end!

[132] Homer A. Kent Jr. *The Expositor's Bible Commentary: Philippians* vol. 11, ed. Frank E. Gaebelein (Grand Rapids: Zondervan, 1978), 126.

BUILDING BRIDGES

A wise bridge builder has

The faith

To emerge from the ranks of mediocrity

The knowledge

To connect distant lands, and

The understanding

Bridges can determine destiny!

Dr. Calvin Glass

APPENDIX A

INTERVIEW QUESTIONS

1. Why are congregations not involved in racial reconciliation programs? If there are congregations with racial reconciliation programs, give personal thoughts about the congregation's plan.
2. What are your personal feelings about race relations within the Christian community and America?
3. What are the reasons that most Christian congregations are not multiethnic?
4. How can building relationships with other races become a congregation's priority?
5. What scriptures relate to racial reconciliation in the Bible?
6. What are the barriers to racial reconciliation within the Christian community and the world?
7. Do you have additional personal concerns and comments concerning racial reconciliation?

APPENDIX B

RACIAL RECONCILIATION BIBLE STUDY

1. What is the scriptural basis for racial reconciliation?

2. What are the biblical blessings connected to racial reconciliation?

3. What are the steps to building positive race relations?
   - Faith
   - Fellowship
   - Friendship
   - Family
   - Forgiveness
     1. Move by faith; this connects individuals to the Family of God (Ephesians 2:8, John 1:11–13).
     2. Make time for fellowship; this compels individuals to spend time with each other (1 John 1:5–7, John 14:23).
     3. Nurture friendships: this constrains individuals to love each other (John 15:12–15).
     4. Acknowledge family; this conforms individuals to do God's will (Matthew 12:46–50).
     5. Demonstrate forgiveness, this corrects and heals individuals and races of people from past hurts, faults, failures, and sins (Ephesians 4:31–32).

4. What are the divine results of racial reconciliation?
   • Favor (Acts 4:32–33)
     1. Embrace favor; this creates God's people as persecuted but blessed influential individuals in society (Acts 4:32–33, Joel 4:9–10).

5. What are the Christian responsibilities to building better relationships within the Body of Christ?
   • A Personal Responsibility (Ephesians 4:1–2)
   • A Spiritual Responsibility (Ephesians 4:3)
   • A Doctrinal Responsibility (Ephesians 4:4–16)
   • A Moral Responsibility (Ephesians 4:17–32)

On my way to a meeting the other day, I ran into a traffic jam where I was at a standstill for over twenty minutes. Then I noticed a car in front of me cut through the grass on my left to get to the other side. Many cars followed this car (including me). I had an urgency and a need to get unstuck and find a new route to get to my destination. As I think of the Ministry of Reconciliation many Christians are stuck and require effective leadership to trailblaze a secure path to fulfill Jesus's prayer for Christian Unity (John 17:20–23).

In this text (the Lord's Prayer, John 17), the Greek word for "one" is *heis* (*hice*), which represents the numeral *1*. It describes the imparted unity that Christ's followers can enjoy. It is based on being in a relationship with other believers demonstrating the life of Christ and possessing the mind of Christ (1 Corinthians 2:16; John 15:5). This is a "vital unity" not based on uniformity but on oneness in nature. Just like God the Father and God the Son are distinct and have different functions but are one in nature, so is the Body of Christ. Paul uses *heis* ten times to describe the unity of the Body of Christ.

   • Romans 12:5–One Body in Christ
   • 1 Corinthians 10:17–One Bread

- 1 Corinthians 10:17–One Body
- Galatians 3:28–One in Christ Jesus
- Ephesians 2:14–Both One
- Ephesians 2:15–One New Man
- Ephesians 2:16–One Body
- Colossians 3:15–One Body

There are additional biblical principles that can be used to fulfill Jesus's burden for unity among believers, we must focus on the following:

6. The **Affect** of Divine Love (1 John 4:11)
7. The **Affirmation** of being "in Christ" (2 Corinthians 5:11–6:2)
8. The **Alignment** of Christ and his Word (1 Corinthians 1:10–19)
9. The **Awareness** of our oneness in Christ (Galatians 3:28–29, Colossians 3:11)
10. The **Agenda** that's empowered by the Holy Spirit (Luke 4:14–21, Matthew 28:17–20, Acts 1:8)

NOTE: The follower of Christ must take on Christ's passion for Christian Unity!

BIBLIOGRAPHY

Asante, Molefi Kete. *Afrocentricity*. Trenton: Africa World Press, Inc., 1991.

Barnes, Albert. *Notes on the New Testament: Explanatory and Practical, Luke and John*. Grand Rapids: Baker Book House, 1957.

_____ *Notes on the New Testament: Explanatory and Practical, Matthew and Mark*. Grand Rapids: Baker Book House, 1958.

Bettenson, Henry and Chris Maunder. *Documents of the Christian Church* 4ᵗʰ ed. New York: Oxford University Press, 2011.

Boa, Kenneth. *Conformed to His Image: Biblical and Practical Approaches to Spiritual Formation*. Grand Rapids: Zondervan, 2001.

Boone, Wellington. *Breaking Through: Taking the Kingdom into the Culture by Out-Serving Others*. Nashville: B & H Publishers, 1996.

Bridges, Charles. *A Modern Study of the Book of Proverbs*. Milford: Mott Media, 1978.

Bromiley, Geoffrey W. *Theological Dictionary of the New Testament*. Grand Rapids: William B. Eerdmans Publishing Company, 1985.

Candlish, Robert S. *Studies in Genesis*. Grand Rapids: Kregel Publications, 1979.

Cannings, Paul. *Making Your Vision A Reality: Proven Steps to Develop and Implement Your Church Vision Plan*. Grand Rapids: Kregel Publications, 2013.

Chafer, Lewis Sperry. *Systematic Theology: Doctrinal Summation* vol. 7. Dallas: Dallas Seminary Press, 1976.

Charles, H. B. Jr. Danny Akins, Juan Sanchez, Richard Caldwell, Jim Hamilton, Owen Strachan, Carl Hargrove, and Christian

George. *A Biblical Answer for Racial Unity.* The Woodlands: Kress Biblical Resources, 2017.

Claerbaut, David. *Urban Ministry.* Grand Rapids: Zondervan Publishing House, 1983.

Clark, Chap and Kara E. Powell. *Deep Justice in a Broken World: Helping Your Kids Serve Others and Right the Wrongs Around Them.* Grand Rapids: Zondervan, 2007.

Cox, Taylor Jr. *Creating Positive Race Relations: What You Can Do to Make a Difference.* Bloomington: WestBow Press, 2020.

Crear, Mark. *The Care and Counsel Bible: Caring for People God's Way.* Nashville: Thomas Nelson, 2001.

Cross, Haman Jr. *Cross Colors: American Christianity in Black and White.* Detroit: Cross Colors, 2015.

Cymbala, Jim and Dean Merrill. *Fresh Wind, Fresh Fire: What Happens When God's Spirit Invades the Hearts of God's People.* Grand Rapids: Zondervan, 2018.

DeYmaz, Mark, and Oneya Fennell Okuwobi. *Multiethnic Conversations: An Eight-Week Journey Toward Unity in Your Church.* Indianapolis: Wesleyan Publishing House, 2016.

Eberhardt, Jennifer L. *Biased: Uncovering the Hidden Prejudice That Shapes What We See, Think, and Do.* New York: Viking, 2019.

Elwell, Walter A. *Evangelical Dictionary of Theology* 2nd ed. Grand Rapids: Baker Book House Company, 2001.

Emerson, Michael O., and Christian Smith. *Divided by Faith: Evangelical Religion and the Problem of Race in America.* New York: Oxford University Press, 2000.

Enns, Paul. *The Moody Handbook of Theology.* Chicago: Moody Publishers, 2008.

Erickson, Millard J. *Christian Theology* 2nd ed. Grand Rapids: Baker Academic, 2009.

Evans, Tony. *Oneness Embraced: Through the Eyes of Tony Evans: A Fresh Look at Reconciliation, the Kingdom, and Justice.* Chicago: Moody Publishers, 2011.

Felder, Cain Hope. *Stony the Road We Trod: African American Biblical Interpretation*. Minneapolis: Fortress Press, 1991.

Fisher, Fred. *Commentary on 1 and 2 Corinthians*. Waco: Word Books, 1977.

Garland, David E. *The New American Commentary: An Exegetical and Theological Exposition of Holy Scripture, 2 Corinthians* vol. 29. Nashville: B & H Publishing, 1999.

Gladding, Samuel T. *Groups: A Counseling Specialty* 7th ed. New York: Pearson, 2016.

Grudem, Wayne. *Systematic Theology: An Introduction to Biblical Doctrine*. Grand Rapids: Zondervan, 2000.

Guthrie, George H. *Hebrews: The NIV Application Commentary, From Biblical Text to Contemporary Life*. Grand Rapids: Zondervan, 1998.

Hayes, J. Daniel. *From Every People and Nation: A Biblical Theology of Race*. Downers Grove: InterVarsity Press, 2003.

Hubbard, David A. *The Communicator's Commentary: Proverbs*. Dallas: Word Books, 1989.

Huang, Jiaxin, Lin Wang, and Jun Xie. "Leader-Member Exchange and Organizational Citizenship Behavior: The Roles of Identification with Leader and Leader's Reputation." *Social Behavior and Personality* 42, no.10 (2014):1699–1712.

Ivery, Curtis L. and Joshua A. Bassett. *America's Urban Crisis and the Advent of Color-Blind Politics: Education, Incarceration, Segregation, and the Future of U. S. Multiracial Democracy*. New York: Rowman & Littlefield Publishers, 2011.

Jennings, Willie James. *The Christian Imagination: Theology and the Origins of Race*. Ann Arbor: Sheridan Books, 2010.

Johnson, Eric L. *God and Soul Care: The Therapeutic Resources of the Christian Faith*. Downers Grove: IVP Academic, 2017.

June, Lee. *Yet with a Steady Beat: The Black Church Through a Psychological and Biblical Lens*. Chicago: Moody Publishers, 2008.

———. *Counseling for Seemingly Impossible Problems: A Biblical Approach*. Grand Rapids: Zondervan, 2002.

Keil, C. F. and F. Delitzsch. *Commentary on the Old Testament: The Pentateuch* vol. 1. Peabody: Hendrickson Publishers, 1989.

Kent, Holmer A. Jr. *The Expositor's Bible Commentary: Philippians* vol. 11. Edited by Frank E. Gaebelein. Grand Rapids: Zondervan Publishing House, 1978.

Lawson, Steven J. *Foundations of Grace: A Long Line of Godly Men* vol. 1. Orlando: Reformation Trust Publishing, 2006.

Malik, Sikandar Hayyat. "A Study of Relationship Between Leader-Behaviors and Subordinate Job Expectancies: A Path-Goal Approach." *Society for Personal Research* 6, no. 2 (2012): 357–371.

McCray, Walter Arthur. *The Black Presence in the Bible and the Table of Nations Genesis 10:1–32: With Emphasis on the Hamitic Genealogical Line from a Black Perspective.* Chicago: Black Light Fellowship, 1990.

McNeil, Brenda Salter. *Roadmap to Reconciliation 2.0: Moving Communities into Unity, Wholeness, and Justice.* Downers Grove: IVP, 2015.

Moore, Russell D., and Andrew T. Walker. *The Gospel and Racial Reconciliation.* Nashville: B & H Publishing Group, 2016.

Nicoll, W. Robertson, *The Expositor's Greek Testament* vol. 2. Grand Rapids: William B. Eerdmans Publishing Company, 1990.

Ogilvie, Lloyd John. *Drumbeat of Love: The Unlimited Power of the Spirit as Revealed in the Book of Acts.* Waco: Word Books, 1980.

Serven, Doug. *Heal Us, Emmanuel: A Call for Racial Reconciliation, Representation, and Unity in the Church.* Oklahoma City: White Blackbird Books, 2016.

Shuler, Clarence. *Winning the Race to Unity: Is Racial Reconciliation Really Working?* Chicago: Moody Publishers, 2003.

Singh, Anneliese A. *The Racial Healing Handbook: Practical Activities to Help You Challenge Privilege, Confront Systemic Racism & Engage in Collective Healing.* Oakland: New Harbinger Publications, 2019.

Smith, Andrea. *Unreconciled: From Racial Reconciliation to Racial Justice in Christian Evangelicalism.* London: Duke University Press, 2019.

Stern, David H. *Jewish New Testament Commentary.* Clarksville: Jewish New Testament Publications, Inc., 1992.

Strong, James. *The New Strong's Concordance of the Bible.* Nashville: Thomas Nelson, 1990.

Tenney, Merrill. *The Expositor's Bible Commentary: The Gospel of John* Vol. 9. Edited by Frank E. Gaebelein. Grand Rapids: Zondervan Publishing House, 1981.

Vines, Jerry. *The Vines Expository Bible.* Nashville: Thomas Nelson, 2018.

Walvoord, John F. *Jesus Christ Our Lord.* Chicago: Moody Press, 1969.

Walvoord, John F. and Roy B. Zuck. *The Bible Knowledge Commentary: New Testament.* USA: Victor Books, 1989.

Woodson, Carter Godwin. *The Miseducation of the Negro.* Lexington: Tribeca Books, 2016.

Wuest, Kenneth S. *Wuest's Word Studies: From the Greek New Testament* Vol. 3. Grand Rapids: Wm. B. Eerdmans Publishing Company, 1973.

Printed in the United States
by Baker & Taylor Publisher Services